A VERY
LONELY

ARSENAL PULP PRESS
Vancouver

PLANET

love, sex, and the single guy

Ryan Bigge

A VERY LONELY PLANET
Copyright © 2001 by Ryan Bigge

ARSENAL PULP PRESS
103-1014 Homer Street
Vancouver, B.C.
Canada V6B 2W9
arsenalpulp.com

The publisher gratefully acknowledges the support of the Canada Council for the Arts and the B.C. Arts Council for its publishing program, and the support of the Government of Canada through the Book Publishing Industry Development Program for its publishing activities.

Portions of this book have appeared in different form in the *National Post* ("He's Cookin,'" July 29, 2000), *Saturday Night* ("What's His Sign?" February 2000), *Terminal City* ("An Eye For Details," October 2-8, 1998), *The Peak*, and *Chatelaine*.

Permission to reprint portions of *Advice For Teenagers On How To Act Properly* by Markus Bigge granted by Nepotism Press. Copyright 1956.

Permission to reprint portions of *The Erlenmeyer Flask of Heartbreak* by Gary Bengi granted by Anagram Publishers. Copyright 1965.

Design by Solo
Lonely guy icon designed by Marc Ngui
Printed and bound in Canada

CANADIAN CATALOGUING IN PUBLICATION DATA:
Bigge, Ryan, 1973-
  A very lonely planet

  ISBN 1-55152-094-X – ISBN 1-55152-108-3 (variant cover)

  1. Single men-Psychology. 2. Single men-Attitudes. 3. Man-woman relationships. I. Title.
HQ800.3.B54 2001   305.38'9652   C2001-910456-1

For Sascha,
Whenever I May Find Her

Acknowledgments

Thanks to Mom and Dad and Oma and the rest of the Bigge clan for their love and support.

Cheers to Blaine and Brian at Arsenal Pulp Press for putting up with me.

A bigge hug for my fond friend Leza Maloney (we'll always have Montreal).

Thanx to the original *Single Guy* cabal: Bryan Raiser, Darren Gawle, Graeme Scott, Craig Huxtable, Mat X, Kevin, Sean, Tony Lee, Andrew Gregory Scratch, Darren Atwater, and Spiff.

Winks for Sascha, Sharon, Katrin, Rachel, Lorraine, Soph, Natalie, Mirah, and Sheila.

Nods to Kalle Lasn, Chris Dixon, *Adbusters*, Brian Salmi, Murray Miller, Nicholas Johnson, Terry Sunderland, Sarmishta, Darby Romeo, Hollis Hopkins and D-code, Danielle, Shireen, CGP, Angela Kozminuk, Elta, Erin Kinghorn, Jen Angel, Jessica Gruner, Jason McLean, *This*, Mark Slutsky, Pi, George Vanous, Kevin Connolly, Taesia, Maria-Suzanne, Patti Pasten, Christine Cosby, R. Seth Friedman, Hal Niedzviecki, *Broken Pencil*, Maria Armstrong, Felix, Julie, Margie, Adam, *Terminal City*, Steve, Lotus, the Magic Eightballs and the MYUBL.

My lighter is held aloft for the honorary Plantains: Ryan Schmidt, Barb Choit, Bryan Tesan, M-strain, and Landscape Body Machine.

Enourmous praise for those who commented on early drafts: Jim Munroe, Bruce Grierson, Graeme Scott, Martina Lang, Steve Wortman, Les Smith, Jeff Chapman, Jason Anderson (music consultant), Jessica Westhead, Bert Archer (idea guy), Emily Pohl-Weary (feminist advisor), Rob Elliott (cocktail nation expert), Patricio Davila, and Ryan McCullah.

Kudos to Gord McLaughlin (*Cooking For Love* editor) and Lawrence Muckerman (humor scrubber).

A tip o' the hat to Daniel J. Collins (photographer extrodinaire), Dean Allen (flower cover), Rosalee Hiebert (flower photographer), Rick Brush (flower model), Terry Lau/ Beehive Design (condom cover), Marc Ngui (icon artist), Greg White (condom photographer/ friend), Red Design, and everyone in the book cover focus group.

For anyone I omitted, either by accident or by intention, I offer a sincere whoops. Thank you very much [insert your name here] for everything you've done. I couldn't have done it without you.

CONTENTS

Single Guys:
First Impressions

Boy Meets Girl. Boy Loses Girl. Boy Writes Book.
14

I Gotta See About a Girl
20

Past, Present, and Accounted For:
Single Guys Through the Ages

You Mock My World
34

Don't Look Back in Anger
39

Wavy Gravy Stain
48

Isn't It Ironic? Not Really
55

The Business of Pleasure
67

Mono Sapien:
Single Guys in Profile

XY Chemistry 101
78

Some Quintessential Single Guys
91

Language of Love Spoken Most Excellently Here: Communication
97

Single Minded: Emotional Rescue
104

Marriage Has Teeth and Him Bite Hot
111

Divine Intervention
116

Sad Bastards of Young: Music
123

Stuck in Second Gear: Friends
137

Escape Plans:
Single Guys on the Lam

Role Models
142

(Im)Personals
148

I Left My Heart in New York: Blind Dates
153

My Homework Was Never Quite Like This: High School
159

Slaving Over a Hot Date: *Cooking for Love*
162

He Blinded Her With Science
167

Pay to Play
171

Single Guys:
We Need to Talk

It Doesn't Have to Be the End of the World
176

Margaret donned thick black rubber gloves that extended well past the elbows of her long slender arms and stepped purposefully towards the tank of electric eels. She grabbed one of the shocking serpents of electric malevolence and quietly approached her boyfriend and co-worker Jake Shields. Jake looked up from the slide he was preparing for the extra-powerful atomic microscope that the SuperTech company had recently acquired, only to see a frightening, Medusa-esque Margaret advancing upon him with the eel. His trembling fear was hidden somewhat by his oversized white lab coat.

"We have to talk," Margaret said, the intensity of a mad woman etch-a-sketched upon her pupils.

Jake quivered like discount gelatin subjected to a 5.3 Richter scale earthquake. "Okay," he offered meekly.

"We need to see other people. By which I mean, it's over. Sorry." Margaret then pretended to throw the eel at Jake before concluding, "I really hope we can still be friends."

      – from *The Erlenmeyer Flask of Heartbreak*
        by Gary Bengi

Love is like a snowmobile racing across the tundra and then suddenly it flips over, pinning you underneath. At night, the ice weasels come.

– Matt Groening, *Love is Hell*

SINGLE GUYS

first impressions

BOY MEETS GIRL.
BOY LOSES GIRL.
BOY WRITES BOOK.

I don't mean to brag, but I've been single for a long time. I'm still not entirely sure why, but loneliness has followed me my whole life – in bars and cars, on moving sidewalks, at frogurt outlets – *everywhere*.

The most frustrating aspect of single life isn't the lack of female companionship (although it's a very close second) but my inability to pinpoint why I don't interact with women like other guys. Perhaps I was a *naïve* (Latin for stupid) teenager, but as a friendly giant (six-foot-five) I assumed that having two-thirds of the tall, dark, and handsome combination would unlock a lot of bedroom doors. Or at the very least, make it easier to meet women of a similar altitude. Or any women at all.

It turned out I was *extremely* naïve. I repeatedly banged my romantic shins during high school and early college. Finally, in the fall of 1993, I began dating a long-time crush and thought the worst was over.

She dumped me a few months later.

To help deal with the Sturm und Drang, I began publishing *Single Guy Zine*, a Xeroxed magazine filled with short essays, Cosmo-like quizzes for men, cartoons, bad advice, quotations about love, music reviews, and intentionally terrible poetry. Through the zine I discovered other guys (and even a few women) who identified with my woebegone persona: a motley crew of sensitive males, politically correct university students, angst-ridden teenage boys, weepy twenty-something indie-rock sad-sacks, divorcées, and widowers.

What publishing a zine taught me, other than how to rip

off Kinko's, was that amidst the fear and self-loathing there are laughs. Short, bitter laughs. But laughs nonetheless. It turned out I was good at being single. My circulation ballooned to nearly 300, and I received favorable reviews from zine guides *FactSheet Five* and *Broken Pencil*. Beyond validating my existence and my wacky theories (read: rationalizations) about the advantages of single life, the zine was cheaper than alcohol and far more effective than therapy.

The fact that it irritated my ex-girlfriend was a nifty bonus.

In the spring of 1997, I published the final issue of *Single Guy Zine*. I stopped because I felt I had exhausted the topic and because the zine had become more curse than blessing. I admit *Single Guy* was meant to be self-promotion of the most obvious kind – unlike this book – but I discovered that most women who read the zine found it simultaneously charming and concerning. In our society, being single isn't something to proudly advertise, but a shameful condition to keep concealed.

Somehow, in the fall of 1997, I again managed to be unsingle for a few months. I have been unattached since. And so, like any normal person, I asked myself some very difficult questions:

> » If I'm so wonderful, why am I still single?
> » What is wrong with me?
> » What are you doing later tonight?

The answers have been slow in coming. Clearly, I'm not unwonderful, so I decided I hadn't explored single life completely. Conveniently, my Eureka! moment occurred a few weeks later.

In the summer of 1998, I discovered that the density of a

given metal could be determined by the amount of water it displaced. No, wait, that was Archimedes.

I discovered the Very Lonely Planet: a hypothetical mental space that single men occupy. Because of the overpowering emotions this mental state provokes, it can sometimes feel like a real, distinct geographical entity. The Very Lonely Planet was a little like those heliocentric models of the universe – a bit clumsy, lacking in celestial precision, but a functional guide to how the world worked.

Many single guys see other guys just like themselves having successful relationships and wonder what god they've angered. When everybody but you is dating, kissing, and getting married, it's reasonable (or at the very least convenient) to believe that you're from another planet.

A very unpopular planet.

For those still confused by the Very Lonely Planet, here are a few metaphors, incorporating varying degrees of pop-culture sophistication, to help elucidate:

> » It is a kind of *Gilligan's Island* populated by unlucky single men whose attempts at escape are elaborate, unintentionally humorous, and rarely successful.
> » Whoa! Dude, it's like *The Matrix*.
> » It is Narnia, a parallel universe that affords some escape from real-world trauma, minus the talking animals and the elaborate wardrobe requirements.

The best metaphor for the Very Lonely Planet, however, is the fugue state, a rare kind of amnesia caused by severe mental trauma. The affected person usually leaves his hometown, and after relocating, is unable to remember his past. He will then adopt a completely new identity and occupation. This situation can last for years, and when the fugue finally ends, the sufferer often can't remember what happened.

The Very Lonely Planet as fugue state works for two reasons: 1) Severe mental trauma corresponds to the pain of being dumped or having to deal with heaps and heaps of unrequited love. 2) Whenever single men finally find a girlfriend, they quickly deny the existence of the Very Lonely Planet, wanting to distance themselves from this village of the damned. We're all familiar with buddies who disappear inside a relationship and become former buddies. So why can't single men have an alternate universe to call their own? A little planet where nobody knows their name?

After "discovering" the Very Lonely Planet, I decided to explore it and map its terrain. The result is this book: a historical, philosophical, biological, epistemological, ontological, and psychological guide to single guys. I hope this book will spackle a noticeable gap in our understanding of gender issues, because if there is one demographic that continues to be vastly underreported and underdescribed by the mainstream media, it is single, mostly white, middle-class males.

Okay, okay, so perhaps guys have hogged the spotlight for the past million years or so. But it's usually a certain kind of male doing the hogging. Hiding in the shadow of the stereotypical football fanatic or date rapist is a fellow I've dubbed the Astute Brute. We know very little about this curious creature, yet Astute Brutes are the dominant nationality of the Very Lonely Planet.

Most universities feature women's studies; think of this book as single guy studies. We are worthy of closer examination, because reflected in our inability to find a mate are the changes of society at large. There are many valid, external reasons for our lack of companionship. I, for example, blame:

» chaos theory and that damn butterfly flapping its wings in India
» my technique of tripping a woman and asking, "How about it?"
» my decision to break a chain letter back in '89
» excess fluoride in the water supply
» the wolves that raised me

Since 1995, women have been able to purchase *The Rules*. Single men are still trying to create their own blueprint for success. Either we have failed to learn the rules of communicating with the opposite sex, or we've decided not to follow them (at our peril), or we don't particularly like the rules and want some new ones, or there are no rules and anarchy reigns supreme.

This book is an attempt to tease out our inner logic and dissect it. You will notice the book is divided into three sections. Do not be alarmed. The first section, **Past, Present, and Accounted For,** describes what a Very Lonely Planet might look like and examines single guys through the ages, so as to better understand our current predicament. This section also puts postmodernism, capitalism, and business culture under the monocle to see how these "isms" have affected dating and mating.

The second section, **Mono Sapien**, sketches the character of the Astute Brute and postulates a periodic table of testosterone viscosity, showing how varying the amount of brain and brawn generates different types of single guys. I then look at some Astute Brute exemplars and examine their communication abilities, probe their emotional stability, and question their spiritual beliefs. Finally, I ransack the Astute Brute's CD rack and audit his interpersonal skills.

The final section, **Escape Plans**, proposes some role models to learn nonsingleness from, before taking a cynical look at the most popular methods of leaving the Very Lonely Planet once and for all.

Every few years an advice columnist emerges to help people figure out the socio-sexual zeitgeist. The 1990s bequeathed us Anka Radakovich, Josey Vogels, Sue Johansen, Rhona Raskin, and Dr. (ecch!) Laura. Oh, and the incredibly popular Dan Savage, who appeals to middle-America's deep-seated desire to have a flippant gay man tell them how to live their lives.

Now, I'm not advertising myself as the next Dan Savage or Dr. (ecch!) Laura. What distinguishes me from nearly every other advice columnist in history is that I urge you to ignore much of what I have to say. After nearly five consecutive years of singleguydom, you'll probably benefit from doing the exact opposite. My best advice is to mope during your early twenties, publish a zine for a few years, mope some more, write a book, and hope that authors become as popular as rock stars.

What I can promise, however, is to treat readers with the dignity and compassion they deserve. I might be occasionally self-deprecating, but this book is not *Sex and Dating for Dummies*. Gallows humor is one thing, being callous is quite another.

I also promise sincerity, as evinced by my suggestion to ignore my advice outright. This isn't Disney treacle, nor an airy-fairy New Age nightmare like *Mars and Venus Meet Abbott and Costello*. It's an open and honest look at why some men are single. Let's begin by categorizing some of the emotional scars I have received in the battle between the sexes.

I GOTTA SEE
ABOUT A GIRL

So, how does someone stay single for five years? An excellent question. Unlike prison, single guys aren't given a parole hearing. Each day we falsely assume we'll be released from singledom, but slowly the weeks turn into months turn into years turn into tears.

Normal men call their ex-girlfriends to help make sense of their present plight. This is my best approximation. Sadly, it's not the first time I've catalogued my shame. The final *Single Guy Zine* (an espionage-themed issue), featured a lengthy article titled "The Secret Report of Agent 006." It was a detailed list of the women I'd loved and lost. In the introduction I wrote:

> This is an extensive dossier of my activities over the past few years, under the rubric **Operation Singled Out**. Hopefully this will help explain how, despite my best intentions, each encounter ended in failure. A brief word about my target female for this mission: my ideal "Bond" girl would be a non-smoking, tall, intelligent, attractive, and musically knowledgeable individual who likes Pina Coladas and getting caught in the rain. Barring height, these traits are negotiable. (I've discovered that an already awkward procedure is made somewhat easier when the mommy and daddy parts nearly align.) Lamentably, I have been continually frustrated in my attempts to find someone matching the above description.

Upon reflection, this was clearly eccentric behavior. But the article is a seminal document in the Bigge canon. Covering December 1993 to February 1997, my "Secret Report" allowed me the opportunity to examine my dating patterns and the problems therein. I discovered that relationships failed because the woman in question:

> » only wanted to be friends
> » was a mermaid who opted to live under the sea after our third date
> » wasn't single
> » was eaten by a tiger
> » didn't meet my occasionally arbitrary list of must-have traits
> » didn't have an airtight alibi for the night of April 6, 1995
> » liked me, but I didn't realize it until it was too late
> » faked her own death
> » was the right person at the wrong time
> » disliked my habit of shouting "Victory for the Forces of Democratic Freedom" at the most inopportune moments
> » didn't want to jeopardize our professional relationship
> » turned out to be my father, Darth Vadar
> » read *Single Guy Zine* and panicked
> » had an "operation"
> » seemed interested but was always "too busy"

I'm proud to report that since the spring of 1997, I have been making a completely different set of mistakes, which I will soon discuss. Beyond the obvious rubbernecking opportunities, I feel that by providing a comprehensive inventory of no-nos, single guys will have a better idea of what not to do. Still, there is something to be said for experience – it allows you to recognize mistakes when you make them a second time.

It will be helpful to break my romantic incarceration into some arbitrary eras:

> » high school (1989-1991)
> » college (1991-1994)
> » the university/zine years (December 1994-February 1997)
> » the post-university/zine years, further subdivided into:
>   • August 1997-May 1999: living on my own in Vancouver
>   • June 1999-present: living in Toronto

While the following list of near-misses (anonymity has been carefully secured) might appear unethical, I'm only committing half of the kiss-and-tell sin. Ultimately, I suffer most from divulging this information. Either future prospects will insist on non-disclosure agreements, or I'll be forced to provide a first date Miranda Warning:

> You have the right to remain silent and refuse to answer any questions. Anything you say or do may appear in my next book. Now that I have advised you of your rights, are you willing to initiate a relationship with me without an attorney present?

Here, then, is my two-bits' worth.

My pre-zine dating recollections are hazy, since "The Secret Report" wisely decided not to trace my courtship history back to the womb. From what I can remember, I was nerdy, awkward, bookish, flippant, funny, and heavy-set during High School. I had no fashion sense worth mentioning. There were some crushes, some tentative attempts at dating, a few sock-hop slow dances, anonymous Valentines, but basically, I was Brian (Anthony Michael Hall's character) from *The Breakfast Club*.

College is a place where adult identity formation occurs. You experiment with different ideaologies. You ask yourself difficult questions:

> » Plato or Socrates?
> » Karl Marx or Adam Smith?
> » Betty or Veronica?

In the first year or so of college I pursued two amazing women who, at the time, were in relationships. While this was painful and frustrating, it did provide some valuable lessons about being chummy with a woman you fancy. It never seems to work.

In the spring of 1993 I met The Most Fantastic Woman in the Whole World™ and in the fall, we dated for an all-too-brief interval. It eventually emerged that she wasn't The Most Fantastic Woman in the Whole World™ an opinion based mainly upon the fact that she broke up with me.

Seven years later (but who's counting), the whole incident feels distorted and distant – nostalgia as viewed through a front door pinhole. At the time, of course, it was the worst thing ever. In my darkest hours I contemplated writing some poetry. The sorrows of young Ryan eventually subsided, and I am now able to laugh about it, but back then the pain blinded me to a few rebounds, like a former stripper turned college student who seemed interested in me in the Spring of 1994 (I swear this is true). She was older than me – coo coo ca-choo – and at the time, this was a big deal (her twenty-five to my twenty). You'd think a man with a nearly empty social calendar would embrace a May-December romance, but you'll excuse me for feeling a little intimidated.

While the stripper certainly didn't fit the stereotype of a dumb blonde who removed her clothing for cash – not that I was planning to pay her – I demurred, hoping instead to win back the heart of The Most Fantastic Woman in the Whole World™

I was also at the height of my "paralysis through analysis" stage of dating, which didn't help matters. (Should I date an ex-stripper? Could I date an ex-stripper? Why would an ex-stripper want to date me?) I stopped short of giving a questionnaire to prospective partners, but clearly I was looking for the ideal woman, somehow overlooking the fact that I was far from perfect.

In the Fall of 1994 I encountered the reverse situation. I met a seventeen-year-old (I was now twenty-one) who went to Catholic school and "had" to wear the uniform. Unfortunately, I learned that the knee-socks come with a Catch-22 – they often can't be removed because some dude named God said so. My forthright admission that I was an atheist made me simultaneously intriguing and repelling, but it was a spiritual chasm she ultimately could never bridge.

How did I met a seventeen-year-old in the first place? In a swimming instructor course. During the summer of 1994 I started working out and taking the courses required to become a lifeguard. It wasn't like *Baywatch* (I wanted to work at an indoor pool), but my new fitness regime meant I could now take my shirt off in public without small children pointing and laughing.

Life improved once I transferred from College to University. The first issue of the zine debuted in December 1994, and the second appeared in March of 1995. I had finally found something worthwhile about being single. As well, I was now working at a swimming pool. The scoresheet tallied well. Pros: I had lost a lot of weight, I had a good-paying job, and the female-male employee ratio was sixty-five to thirty-five percent. Cons: I had a goatee and ostentatious 1950s black-framed glasses.

Unfortunately, my self-esteem never quite caught up with my new physique and I walked around like Mr. Magoo most of the time. Yet I nearly escaped the Very Lonely Planet in the spring of 1995. It was then I met a lovely young lady at university. Unfortunately, during our initial meeting, I was given the erroneous impression that she had a boyfriend. So I hung out with her occasionally. I loaned her some indie-rock albums. I sent her lots of witty e-mail. All the while thinking she had a boyfriend. In retrospect, this relaxed, easygoing charm was probably quite endearing.

By the time I discovered she was single, final romantic deliberations had begun regarding myself and another guy. I ended up with a set of steak knives.

In the late summer of 1995 I met a cute gal who quite liked me. However, she was very religious – much more so than the seventeen-year-old. I tolerate low levels of religiosity, provided it isn't crammed down my throat. I liken it to smoking. A couple of cigarettes per year (i.e., Easter and Christmas) is okay. But from all reports, she was chain smoking three packs of God a day. Worse, she didn't have a schoolgirl uniform, so I decided I couldn't be her Adam.

In retrospect, I met many women during 1995. Eleven by my calculations. Some had no potential, some had plenty. The law of averages should have worked in my favor, but didn't. Dating is not a smooth, simple exercise. It instead resembles a Choose-Your-Own-Adventure (If you try and kiss the princess, turn to page 15. If you order a meal with garlic, turn to page 235).

By late 1995 I had a weekly show at the university radio station. I became friendly with one of the station employees. She was bright, funny, and lesbian. Another male might have bemoaned his bad luck, but given my *Single Guy Zine* career, this made perfect sense. We engaged in some harmless flirting. Or so I thought.

In February of 1996 it was revealed that she wasn't lesbian but bisexual. And she liked me. This information arrived a few weeks before she was to depart on a lenghty journey. I learned I can't make snap decisions. I had no time to step back and reflect. To paraphrase the situation from my perspective, she was saying, "Try not to feel pressured by the fact that a lapsed lesbian has put her faith in the male race, and you happen to be the chosen one." I was having enough trouble dealing with the fact that she had a pierced tongue.

I would like to say that I handled the situation with dignity and aplomb. To my credit, I eventually (two years later) apologized for retreating like a frightened turtle. But I'm definitely overdrawn at the First National Bank of Karma.

The worst part of the experience is knowing I was only a year or so away from seeing *Chasing Amy*. I have reservations about putting "profound insight" and "Kevin Smith" in the same sentence, but *Chasing Amy* taught me something very valuable – a woman who has sampled the thirty-one flavors at Baskin Robbins is more likely to be happy with Vanilla Ryan. If I ever meet another lesbian who turns out to be bisexual, I promise to act flattered instead of flummoxed.

Later that spring, I made a huge breakthrough. Occasionally, if a man is genuinely disinterested in a woman, the woman will try five times harder to get his attention. This is the sort of Murphy's Law that makes single guys seriously consider life as a monk.

As the post-university era began, life held much promise. In the fall of 1996 I became managing editor of *Adbusters* magazine. In January of 1997 I completed the final issue of *Single Guy Zine*, a decision designed to end my losing streak. (A few weeks later I went bowling on a first date, proving I still had a lot to learn.) And in the summer of that year, I left the suburban nest and moved into an apartment in beautiful downtown Vancouver.

I had two roommates: a tall blonde woman and a tall bottle-blond man (I had to dye my hair as a condition of the lease). The tall blond man was a swinger cast from the Vince Vaughn mold, and did his best to help me out. Despite living on my own, despite trading my teddy bear for a bearskin rug, female traffic in my lair was light.

Soon after moving downtown, I met up with an old high school friend named Leanne. I had a crush on her that could be traced back to Grade 10 (1988). She is tall and smart and funny and refined and ambitious and very attractive and . . . well, listen to me prattle on. To prove her impeccable taste, she was as fascinated with *Twin Peaks* as I was during high school.

During Grade 12, I tried, in my pathetic and gangly manner, to let her know I liked her, without ever actually saying so aloud. My assumption was that she found my attempts endearing but ultimately repulsive.

So, anyway, in the summer of 1997 we meet up. *She makes me dinner.*

Then we decide to go for a walk. *We go to the beach*. It's raining lightly, and we meander along the train tracks. She is wearing a cute little yellow raincoat. I am slowly getting soaked because I lack an umbrella or a hoodie. The only thing missing is a mariachi band following, at a discreet distance, on a hand-pump car.

Despite the environmental cues, I've entered the whole rendezvous with zero expectations. I have no desire to get my hopes up again. I'm acting like the friendliest friend in friendville. The mayor of Chum City.

So we're walking along, and she says, "It's really weird hanging out with you, Ryan Bigge."

"Why is that?" I ask.

"Well, if I was hanging out with [insert name of mutual acquaintance] after not seeing him for a few years, it would be perfectly normal, because we were good friends in high school. But with you it's different because I had a crush on you in high school."

With one sentence, Leanne instantaneously rewrote my biography. This was a fairly momentous admission, and I needed some time to process the fact that The Most Fantastic Woman in the Whole World™ had – at one point – actually liked me. Here was the all-time classic single guy fantasy brought to life. Unfortunately, no one ever told me what to do if it actually occurs. Probably because it only happens in the movies.

I should have done something dramatic – a quick burst of machismo. Kiss her, for example.

I did not. Hindsight is 20-20.

Instead, I mentioned that I, too, had a crush on her in high school, and we continued walking as if *nothing had happened*. During our next meeting/date, when I asked how she felt

28

about me now, she avoided the question. I think by not seizing the appropriate opportunity, I disappointed her. She walked me to the edge of the cliff, but I refused to take a leap of faith. I've come to accept that I'm smart like tractor when it comes to dealing with women.

The postscript: she's now married. To someone who is not me. Not to get all philosophical, or worse, raise the specter of *Back to the Future*, but it's strange to think how different my life might be if I'd busted a move on the choo-choo tracks. Perhaps she would now be Leanne Bigge and you wouldn't be reading this book. My loss is your gain.

Things improved in the fall of 1997, when I managed to figure out that a woman I had been flirting with for a while liked me. We dated for a few months, but she was very busy with her Masters thesis and wanted something casual. Starving men should never pretend to enjoy a crust of bread.

In February 1998, six months after moving downtown, and right on schedule, I developed a Completely Futile, Never To Be Verbalized Crush On My Female Roommate. This phenomenon occurs in ninety percent of the single male population, despite constant and convincing denials to the contrary. These temporary obsessions generally evaporate within sixty days, and are perfectly harmless, provided you never, ever mention them while you and she live under the same roof.

Otherwise, the first half of 1998 wasn't great. A woman with potential announced a week after I met her that she was going to Europe for three months. I had another brush with an older woman. And the usual cavalcade of misplaced crushes.

In the fall of 1998, something so unbelievable occurred (no, not what you're thinking) that I'd prefer to leverage the suspense. Suffice to say, it involves New York, a fax machine, and Elle MacPherson. Stay tuned.

In November, I met a bright, attractive woman at a party. I even found the courage to ask for her number. I called her up, and we eventually went for coffee. I say eventually, because she was very busy. The "busy" plea is always difficult to interpret, since a woman who's infatuated with a guy will invariably make time to be with him. In her case, she had a demanding job and an active social life. But the distinction between playing hard-to-get and sitting in the bleachers can be very subtle. Hectic gals remind me of slot machines, since they both operate on a variable-ratio schedule of reinforcement – pester her often enough and you'll get a date. One-armed bandits pay out after a certain number of attempts (say on average, every tenth pull), which means sometimes you only have to spin once, and sometimes you have to deal with a bunch of lemons. A variable-ratio schedule of reinforcement is very effective at keeping gamblers hooked, and pigeons will peck a response key several hundred times a minute on said schedule. This is where all the problems with persistence versus stalking start for single guys.

I'm proud to say that I didn't do anything stupid – I simply gave up. Besides, I had other things on my mind. In the spring of 1999, I decided to move to Toronto. I felt that announcing this decision ahead of time would prompt any Vancouver women secretly pining for me to speak now or forever hold their peace. The silence was deafening.

Oh yeah. In January I had another brush with "the guy acting aloof makes woman much more interested in him." I managed to squander home turf advantage yet again.

The Toronto era was tumultuous. I arrived in the big city, wide-eyed, clutching a twenty-kilogram suitcase that represented my vain attempt to Tetris the spiritual and material essence of my twenty-six years into a Samsonite. I had moved to seek my fortune as a freelance writer. I focused on earning enough money to live and getting settled career-wise. In late September I met a fantastic young woman, a writer of fiction, but I convinced myself I wasn't quite ready for a relationship. I had a good reason. I'm an idiot.

The first half of 2000 was also fairly quiet, until June, when I appeared on a television dating game show called *Cooking for Love*. I won't bore you with the particulars.

And then, in August of that year....

Sorry, no happy endings. If this book were a true romantic comedy, despite my ineptitude and a hilarious cameo by Don Knotts, I would fall in love with The Most Fantastic Woman in the Whole World™ in August of 2000. But this book is heavy on the comedy, light on the romance, meaning that even if I had met a woman matching this description, we would have agreed to breakup in February of 2001, a few days before my birthday.

Which just happens to be Valentine's Day.

PAST, PRESENT, AND ACCOUNTED FOR

single guys through the ages

YOU MOCK
MY WORLD

The Very Lonely Planet is a bunch of electrical impulses bouncing through the dendrites and axons of single guy synapses, a dreadful world contained safely within the cranium. After many years of painstaking research, I have converted these thought patterns into their architectural equivalents. I recently built a scale-model version of the Very Lonely Planet out of Lego. So let's treat the Very Lonely Planet as an actual place, to make it a little easier to understand what I'm going on about. As with the *Planet of the Apes*, this celestial body populated by single guys will eventually turn out to be Earth. Call me Cornelius.

Men are transported to a Very Lonely Planet on North By Northwest Airlines, who run a fleet of single-engine planes. Their aircraft feature cramped seats, food with all the fruity nuance of soggy brown cardboard, wistful in-flight movies like *Casablanca* or *The Lonely Guy*, and safety cards detailing how not to commit suicide. And, of course, there are absolutely no female flight attendants. You can, however, drink as much as you wish while on board. It won't improve your holiday, but it might help you forget some of it.

Regardless of arrival time, all flights are red-eyes. Your "We have to talk" travel voucher will appear to be one-way. Most visits are inconveniently scheduled and terribly unexpected. Travelers bring lots of emotional baggage.

I have yet to be greeted at the Very Lonely Planet International Airport by a woman in a muumuu offering a lei. The best anyone can hope for is a wilted black rose blithely thrown by some guy in scruffy jeans. There will be no chauffeur with a cardboard sign advertising your name in magic marker. There might be a woodcut figure of a man holding his hands a metre apart with a thought bubble that reads, "You must be this depressed to enter."

Picture the Very Lonely Planet as if it were a theme park, minus the fun. It is devoid of birds. There are no bees. It features a color scheme similar to Edvard Munch's painting *The Scream*. In fact, the gift shops sell gaudy inflatable versions of the screaming guy, along with poetry and Kool-Aid. I prefer the latter. As dead German philosopher Martin Heidegger put it: "Poetry ist krap." Despite my naysaying, poesy is very popular. There are three main kinds of poetry for sale. The Really Terrible kind:

> *"Love"*
> *You are the ocean,*
> *I am the shore.*
> *Though you occasionally rub me the wrong way.*

The Really, Terribly, Pretentious kind:

> *"Untitled"*
> *White swan*
> *eating*
> *a black rose*
> *choking on*
> *the thorns.*
> *Ouch!*

And the Haiku kind (which is slightly less terrible due to the necessary concision):

> *The pretty girls are*
> *everywhere; I want to see*
> *their underwear. Please.*

Single guy theme park mascots include Charlie Brown, Holden Caulfield, and Nintendo's Mario. Visitors travel by unicycle or monorail. Everyone eats at the Nighthawks Café, home of the Woody Allen Burger, which features extra malaise and a semi-secret sauce. Those in a rush grab an Unhappy Meal. Calorie counters nosh on a tossed salad with vinaigretteful dressing, which contains eleven herbs and spices (hate, envy, lust, malice, anger, betrayal, avarice, saline, bile, regret, and paprika).

Very Lonely Planet supermarkets sell specialty products such as Men's Pocky (crispy pretzel dipped in dark chocolate for the intelligent connoisseur who enjoys the finer points in life), Masters and Johnson's As Few Tears As Humanly Possible Shampoo, and Calvin Klein's Lost Cause For Men (a perfume designed to mask the acrid aroma of desperation). There is also Crazy About You Glue ("Reach out and touch someone . . . permanently") and Little Blank Books for female phone numbers. Dignity cannot be purchased anywhere in the Very Lonely Planet, since the laws of supply and demand are strictly enforced.

The lonely lending library features books such as *Love is Hell* by Matt Groening and *Bonobo, The Forgotten Ape* by Frans De Waal and Frans Lanting. (If you think traditional apes are frisky, you ain't seen nothing. This is *Brave New World* with simians.) There are also comic books like *Optic Nerve* by Adrian Tomine (no one does aimless, gorgeous twenty-something angst better), and *Jimmy Corrigan: The Smartest Kid on Earth* by Chris Ware (a heart-wrenching tale of Jimmy, a lonely, emotionally-impaired human castaway who meets his father for the first time at age thirty-six). There are even some children's books, including:

> » *Where's Waldo's Girlfriend?*
> » *Curious George and the Dominatrix*
> » *The Locksmith and the Bra Clasp*

At the Very Lonely Planet Imax theatre, you can see *Happiness* (a creepy film with a single guy whose mood is the exact opposite of the title) and *Beauty and the Beast* (a movie in which the ugly guy successfully woos the woman). Finally, there are daily continuous showings of *Rochelle, Rochelle*, a young woman's strange erotic journey from Milan to Minsk.

The arcade has a Microsoft Home-Office Dating Simulator (go to a *Red Dwarf* convention!) and Microsoft Marriage (marry the woman of your dreams, provided you're a billionaire!). And, of course, *Tomb Raider*. Single guys tend to dislike real women with silicon breasts, since they're unnatural (and unattainable), but a woman generated from silicon chips is another matter entirely. Despite the outrageous cleavage, I believe Ms. Croft is a sophisticated feminist icon. By which I mean she carries a gun.

During the first few days of vacation, guys wear an untucked shirt and old, unwashed jeans. Black clothing is another popular choice. Some guys don't bother getting dressed most days, choosing instead to lounge around in a coffee-stained terrycloth robe.

The scruffy beard is another popular fashion accessory. As hairy single guys are fond of saying, "There's a funny story about this beard ... I'm too depressed to shave."

Most men spend their first few nights at Motel One, which is equipped with everything the nouveau sad-sack may need, including an ambiance-generating dry ice machine. Rooms at the Motel One feature extra-strength EndoTech drywall, which allows you to repeatedly bang your head against it, without damage (to the wall).

Motel One showers have no hot water. All phones are equipped with breathalyzers, which are activated after eleven p.m. in order to prevent the inevitable drunken call.

Wealthy single guys can go down to the end of Lonely Street, and stay at the Heartbreak Hotel. Guests receive a fifty percent discount if they get so lonely they actually die.

The weather report is always the same: raining men.

In the 1950s, the gravitational pull of the Very Lonely Planet was feeble. Since 1960, however, achieving terminal velocity from this accursed orb has become increasingly more difficult. By studying our history, we might be better able to Escape from the Planet of the Very Lonely.

DON'T LOOK BACK IN ANGER

My BA in history (suitable for framing) has taught me the value of learning from our ancestors to better understand the current plight of single men. Or, as historian George Santayana so famously noted, "Those who cannot remember the past are doomed to blah, blah, blah."

I'll begin by looking at the 1950s, the zenith of singleguy-dom, before taking a toboggan ride down the slippery slope into an increasingly complicated world. Certainly, not everything about the 1950s was keen, but there is something to be said for a vibrant social architecture. Repression is bad, but innumerable helpful suggestions about how to live your life are more easily tolerated. We might laugh at all those advice books and social guidance films now, but at least someone was trying to help poor, confused, clueless single men figure out how to meet and treat women.

The Very Lonely Planet became an intellectual construct on February 14, 1950. While singleologists such as Henri Contraire might disagree, it was not until the middle of the twentieth century that men attained, as Marx might have put it, "a singular consciousness." Before this time, there were simply too many other things for single men to worry about (war, prohibition, the Great Depression, Heisenberg's uncertainty principle).

The post-World War II era ushered in an age of Protected Prosperity, since Uncle Sam now had a bomb so big that even he didn't want to detonate it (again). The *Pleasantville* decade was an idyllic time when you didn't have to lock your doors at night, cigarettes didn't yet cause cancer, and black people were held in such high esteem that they had their very own water fountains. And as a special bonus feature, that narrator from *The Wonder Years* would occasionally supply the astute little voice inside your head.

This adult recess gave men an opportunity to reassess their manliness. Unfortunately, most of them didn't bother. Life was good, the economy was booming, and all that spare time and spare change made an extended courtship period possible. Before men could worry too much about the new romantic etiquette, Madison Avenue, with a little help from *Esquire* and *Playboy*, created the bachelor.

Suddenly, there was mood music (*Music for Bachelors* by Henri René and His Orchestra), chi-chi drinks (Tom Collins and Martinis), and romantic crib notes printed on cocktail napkins. ("To be popular with girls, a man must do the wrong thing at the right time.")

But well before Full Spectrum Pan Orthophonic Sound and Tiny Paper Umbrellas were invented, guys had a number of unique rituals and signifiers. During the forties and fifties, they wore hats, shaved with a brush and mug, hung out at the racetrack, played lots of poker, wore sock garters, smoked pipes, carried flasks, puttered in basement workshops, lounged in smoking jackets, and relaxed in rumpus rooms.

The Playboy Advisor and the Esquire Man provided comprehensive lifestyle guidance for this new tribe. It was equal parts philosophy and philandering, designed to create the sort of fellow that no lady could resist. It was a little like the Listerine company, which created halitosis and provided the cure. You're not single, you're a bachelor – a bachelor by choice.

The fifties were short on pathetic single guys because we looked virtually indistinguishable in our grey suits. Aiding the situation were numerous socially-condoned public outlets of expressing sexual frustration, including the wolf whistle, the eyes popping out of the head, and the tongue unfurling like a red carpet onto the floor.

The whole bachelor scam worked in large part because women were happy to oblige. They pretended to be impressed by fire (Zippo lighters and barbecues) and bright shiny objects (cars with tail fins). This created the impression that men were sophisticated scoundrels, even though we were simply following orders.

Women played along because in the 1950s, men acknowledged, either tacitly or explicitly, that marriage was inevitable. They would ultimately settle down, raise a family, buy a pair of black-framed glasses, and do the best damn job they could on the Jenkins account. The "us versus them" mindset towards gender relations was more bluster than reality. In the pre-Pill era, you either became a hermit, a rogue, or engaged. (Homosexuality didn't become really "cool" or "happening" until the mid-sixties.)

Marriage held a certain magic and promise. Everyone else was doing it, and it sure beat jumping off a bridge. Millions strolled down the aisle in an age when you could buy marriage licenses out of gumball machines and both the gum and the marriage would keep their flavor for more than twenty minutes.

Meanwhile, boys too young for *Playboy* were provided with a different set of rules and regulations through the social guidance film. The attempt at social engineering through 16mm celluloid reached its apogee during the 1950s. Films like *What to Do on a Date* and *How Do You Know It's Love?* were meant to inculcate good thoughts and eradicate bad ones. It was all about poise, posture, and pulling taffy.

The effect of these films are certainly arguable, but in retrospect all those sockhops, drive-ins, box socials, and malt shops represented the golden age of courtship. Yes, there were curfews and rules against petting, and the pressure to conform was intense. But this was the first great leap forward in creating an agreed upon set of dating rules since the knights of chivalry developed the Rules of Courtly Love in the twelfth century.

As if those guidance films weren't enough, there were magazine articles and advice books aplenty:

> » *Facts of Life and Love for Teen-Agers* by Evelyn Millis Duvall
> » *Attaining Manhood: A Doctor Talks to Boys About Sex* by George W. Corner
> » *'Twixt Twelve and Twenty: Pat Talks to Teenagers* by Pat Boone
> » *Your Happiest Years* by Dick Clark

Coincidentally, my late grandpa, Markus Bigge, wrote such a book, entitled *Advice for Teenagers on How to Act Properly*. Published in 1956, it garnered several reviews, the most favorable noting, "It is a book with many pages, some of which feature illustrations."

The following *Advice for Teenagers* excerpts provide a revealing look at social morés. Be warned that Markus was, to say the least, rather self-assured about his opinions:

Preface to Success

Hello teenager! I bet you think you've got the world figured out, don't you? Well, I've got news for you. You don't. Not at all. Not one bit. That's what school and other respected institutions are for – they know what's best and aren't afraid to tell you.

But don't despair. Everybody experiences confusion during their teenage years, even respected advice book authors. One day you're walking along, minding your own business when "bang!" crazy changes start occurring and making decisions becomes much more complicated.

I intend to ensure that your decisions are good decisions. Because you see, life is about choices. My choices, your choices, good choices, bad choices. Only when my choices become your choices will you avoid bad choices and select good choices.

The first few chapters are kinda dull, as he discusses how to properly introduce people, how to act at parties, and how to read a "How To" book. But things heat up in Chapter Five (subtitled "Weird Feelings, Weird Thoughts") when he starts talking about the opposite sex:

In high school, or earlier, you will notice changes (wider shoulders, a deepening voice, and wiry facial hair). These changes are caused by hormones. In males, the hormone causing all the kerfuffle is called testosterone. Testosterone is a multi-chained Pyrex molecule that, when mixed with maltshops and movie theatres, produces puberty.

In females, a hormone called estrogen has a few tricks up her delicate, lacy sleeve. Estrogen causes tissue swelling in women which consequently causes tissue swelling in men. This "her"mone also causes physical and emotional changes which are so complex and confusing that they are beyond the scope of this book.

> Suffice it to say, women do not grow facial hair or develop strong urges toward boys. It's only boys who are cursed with desire, a desire that must be kept repressed at all times.

By an incredible coincidence, my grandfather decided to explain these hormones by tracing the successes and failures of Ryan Smith:

> Ryan, a completely fictional character, has recently been "injected" with testosterone by Mother Nature's hypodermic needle and is starting to undergo some Dr. Jekyll and Mr. Hyde-like transformations.
>
> Ryan has decided that his classmate Sue will one day be his wife. Let's observe his stroll down the yellow brick road towards romance and adulthood, and see if he finds a heart, a brain, and courage.
>
> My dear grandmama used to say that "You can't get a cat and a mouse to kiss each other." In the same way, it's nearly impossible to trick a girl into liking you.
>
> Luckily, the key word is nearly. If Ryan follows proper dating etiquette, he should be able to get Sue to agree to a date.

In Chapter Six (subtitled "Ryan Tries to Trick a Girl into Liking Him"), Mr. Smith asks Sue to accompany him to the hayride jamboree. She says yes, but....

> Ryan seemed to do everything right. Or did he? No he did not. He didn't plan ahead.
>
> Ryan assumed Sue would say no — and was so stunned that she said yes — that he didn't bother to ask beforehand if he could borrow his father's car. Planning is the key to having a successful and non-stimulative evening with a girl. As it turns out, Ryan's father Arthur is going out to gather five bushels of radishes from his brother Hank's farm on Saturday evening.

> Even if Arthur hurries home, no God-fearing teenage boy would dare pick up his date in a radish-mobile that smells like the produce aisle – if not worse.

Eventually, Ryan gets the car, and he and Sue go on a date at the pizza parlor. Ryan is unable to think of much to say, and the evening goes poorly. Sue, unlike Ryan, learns from the experience:

> "Ugh." That's what Sue is thinking after that terrible dinner encounter with Ryan. Luckily, it wasn't a complete waste of time. Resourceful Sue compiled a short list of Dating Do's and Do Not's:
>   1) Do not date Ryan.
>   2) See rule #1.
> Next time, if there is a next time, Ryan will need to prepare better. To combat awkward silence, the scourge of all dates, Ryan will have to write out topics of conversation ahead of time on four-by-five recipe cards, to help further big and small talk alike.

Despite the discomfort of their first date and Sue's dating Do Not's, Ryan did pay for Sue's meal. She considers Ryan's request for another meeting with due diligence and eventually accepts his invitation to see *Angry Gorgon Monster Attacks the Mauve Planet* at the local drive-in:

> Soon Ryan and Sue arrive at The Drive-In. Sometimes, The Drive-In can be a very bad place indeed. What many women do not know is that men often get "itchy" when they are alone with their date. Since women do not get "itchy" as often or as rapidly as men, they are often confused by their date's strange behavior.
> It is the female's responsibility to keep things under control during the date. Luckily, Sue's mother

has taught Sue that sex is never enjoyable. However, some girls aren't fortunate enough to have such a wise and helpful role model. For these women, whose decisions could lead them down the path to perdition, I must warn them never to give in to temptation and allow the boy to initiate the commencement of petting.

I cannot stress the ideas of the last paragraph too strongly. NEVER touch your date below the neck. Or above the neck. Petting is *wrong*. This idea is so unthinkable that I've put the word "never" in upper-case and "wrong" in italics. I may underline it next. Or put it in **bold**. I haven't decided yet.

Once you enter Henry Ford's great legacy, Satan is your hitchhiker, impishly grinning and urging you to explore his terribly wicked domain....

Brimstone, hellfire, pitchforks, you get the idea. I'll skip ahead to the inevitable happy ending:

Ryan eventually convinces Sue that marrying him will not be the worst decision she'll ever make. Sue agrees and after they finish high school, they become engaged. They live happily ever after. The end.

Conclusions

What have we learned from Ryan Smith and Sue with no discernible maiden name?

Ryan learned that persistence pays off. He also learned how to use stifling social conventions to his advantage. While he never quite found that brain he was looking for, he discovered his Dorothy, and that's all that matters. (This is what is known as the use of a straw man in an argument.)

Sue learned her mother was right — sex is never enjoyable.

Markus, like so many of his ilk, meant well. Once upon a time, nice girls didn't kiss on the first date and onanism caused visual impairments. Such an era might sound terrible, but the seemingly manageable nature of the fifties holds some appeal. Advice about sex came in two basic formats: Don't Do It and the less popular *Please* Don't Do It. As the narrator from the film *Are You Popular?* solemnly intoned, "Girls who park in cars are *not* really popular."

Life was peachy until October 1957, when the Russians launched Sputnik. Suddenly, eradicating the Soviet threat became far more important than eradicating premarital sex.

If not Sputnik, something else would have accomplished the shift in priorities. Transporting the citizens of post-WWII North America down the highway of abundance in a stodgy Edsel couldn't work forever. Like nutty college sophomores trying to discover how many freshmen could be crammed into a phone booth before it shattered, 1950s society eventually broke free of its moral and political Plexiglas. *Playboy* finally got everyone a little too hot and bothered. People started questioning authority more often in the wake of the quiz show scandals, which revealed that not everything on television was true. After a million years of nearly uncontested patriarchy, things began to slowly unravel. Women wanted more rights and blacks wanted to use the honky's water fountains. The easy-to-follow rules, the power of positive thinking, and the witch-hunt trials of Senator Joseph McCarthy were about to be doused with incense, peppermint, and patchouli.

WAVY GRAVY STAIN

As a member of Generation X, I am required by law to state that I am sick of the sixties. Instead of pretending I have something new or worthwhile to say about The Beatles, JFK, Malcolm X, Woodstock, Vietnam, or Tiny Tim, I will instead examine the major developments in the advice book genre.

In 1962, all heck broke loose when Helen Gurley Brown's *Sex and the Single Girl* was published. The sexual revolution, thanks in large part to The Pill, was changing everything. To give Brown's comments some context, a fifties book like *Blueprint for Teen-Age Living* by William C. Menninger counseled the following:

> There seems to be a lot of confusion about goodnights. The boys claim that the girls expect to be kissed good-night, and the girls say the boys expect to be kissed. As with many aspects of boy-girl relations, the girl is the one who makes the decisions, who controls the situation. This may seem unfair, but that's the way it is.

In *Sex and the Single Girl*, Ms. Brown spoke thusly:

> A married woman who uses sex as a weapon is being a kind of rat. By the traditional covenants of marriage she is supposed to sleep with her husband in return for his giving her his name, a home, an income, and a father for her children. If she blackmails him for dining-room chairs by withholding her body, he has every justification for losing the rent money at poker. A single woman who doesn't deny her body regularly and often to get what she wants, i.e., married or more equitable treatment from her boyfriend, is an idiot.

Social guidance films had two fatal flaws. The first was that their success was predicated on the assumption of ideological invulnerability. The second was that they never wavered from their pre-marital sex policy (that being, "No way!"). So when society shifted seismically, they became irrelevant. The fact that they tried to tackle complex issues in ten minutes didn't help. Thanks to the *ABC Afterschool Special*, we now know that topics such as anorexia and cooties require at least an hour of exploration.

For most of the sixties, everyone went sex-crazy. In 1969, *The Sensuous Woman* by "J" was published ("One of the most arousing things you can do to a man is the Butterfly Flick") as was the classic *Everything You Always Wanted to Know about Sex ~ But Were Afraid to Ask* by David R. Reuben. It's easy to mock these books, but they sold millions of copies and had a clear impact on the general populous.

Not every guy was able to unlearn the moral inflexibility the fifties had instilled, and so not every guy deftly handled the rapid changes of the 1960s. Certainly, the sixties' focus on individuality was a good thing. The suppression of personality so common in the 1950s disappeared. But as it turned out, not every single guy *had* a personality to suppress. The bachelor of the fifties lived in a nice, cloistered world, and now, suddenly, chaos had descended on his empire. Fifties masculinity was a western town in a Hollywood film, a fancy façade with nothing but a few two-by-fours propping it up.

Women's Liberation meant chicks began to make some strides in the workplace. As broads climbed the corporate footstool and neared the glass ceiling – which they were still asked to Windex – they could better afford to wait for the right guy. Or at least the better-than-average guy. *The Sensuous Woman* dared make specific requests (Chapter Ten: "How To

Tell in Advance If a Man Will be a Good Bed Prospect"). Good provider, sure, but also a demon in the sack. Helen Gurley Brown dared mock us guys ("Some men proffer their kisses and propositions with all the finesse of an invading army"). Men started taking those Charles Atlas ads seriously, and staying fashionable became a constant concern. For the first time, there were men who weren't single by choice.

Worse, we discovered that the Space Age Bachelor Pad was infested with termites. The Playboy Philosophy was less Jean-Jacques Rousseau and more David Ogilvy. Hef was concerned with the size of our wallets, not the size of our thoughts. Maintaining our manhood meant owning the newest records, threads, and stereo equipment. We were no longer citizens of a bachelor Shangri-La, but mere consumers; acquisition now trumped attitude.

That 1970s decade was a bit of a bummer. After the turbulent, confusing sixties, it was clear that men required an overarching principle to give their lives meaning. Thus, Eric Weber's 1970 book *How to Pick Up Girls!* Weber was a shy guy who decided to interview a bunch of "terrific-looking" women he dubbed The Fabulous 25. "They're all smart, poised, witty, and good talkers – the kind of girls you'd give at least one of your eye teeth to pick up."

What he did was simple. He asked them how a guy like Weber ("I'm not rich or good-looking") could pick up girls like themselves. Using their responses as the basis of his book, Weber theorized about the art of meeting women, self-published the results, took out some ads in *National Lampoon* and *Penthouse*, and sold a million copies.

Really.

How to Pick Up Girls! is worth analyzing for a number of reasons, not least of which is the fifty bucks it cost to track down a copy. Perhaps more importantly, the book describes something we today take for granted as perfectly normal: the pick-up. Weber defined this procedure as "meeting a woman without being formally introduced to her by a third party." Remember, this book was written when singles bars were a novelty. Weber sets up the historical context thusly: "Twenty years ago you would have been right in assuming it was almost impossible to strike up a relationship with a strange girl. ... That was before The Pill and mini-skirts and see-through blouses and the whole sexual revolution type thing."

This was a great leap forward and a great leap backward for single guys. On the one hand, it increased the opportunities to meet women a hundred-fold. However, if you were a shy guy, you were now at a disadvantage. Previous to this, men most often met women through an aforementioned third party. And quite often, even the most inept single guy could take it from there. Or, as Weber put it, "Let's face it – most guys know how to handle a girl once they've been introduced to her. When you're visiting Aunt Hortense (the family matchmaker) and the cute, busty girl from next door just *happens* to drop by, that's a natural."

How to Pick Up Girls! is an incredible heirloom. In the chapter, "How to Be Sexy," Weber suggests a new wardrobe as one way of strutting your stuff: "[Try] bell bottoms and English boots and wide ties. Wear a body shirt or leather dungarees or a groovy vest. Be dramatic. Leave the top button of your shirt open. Wear shades or those new rimless glasses."

It is easy to find fault with Weber. *How to Pick Up Girls!* is the only best-selling book with an exclamation point I own.

However, much of his advice is still relevant, and I imagine that at the time, it was groundbreaking. He told men that personality trumps appearance. Be yourself. Smile. Be cool. Make her laugh. Act nice. Most importantly, the chapter "Women Get Horny" revealed the best kept secret of the era. "So the next time you're wondering whether to try to pick up a certain girl, remember: it may be a long time since she's been to bed with a man. She may be horny. Very Horny. Right at that very moment."

The book is dense with sexism, and it's encouraging to realize things got somewhat better during the next thirty years. In the chapter "How to Get Women to Pick You Up," he notes, "Even with Women's Lib coming into its own, it's going to be a long time before the average chick can approach a strange man without feeling like a whore." Regardless of how we might view the book today, this is a seminal work in the evolution of the single guy. It continues to sell well (there is a *How to Pick Up Girls 2000!* edition) with only slight revisions.

The new rules reflected a new mindset, and gone were the chaste goals of hearty handholding. This was the dawning of the age of the one-night stand. And this development created some problems for single guys who were too disgusted or too scared to try the nine-hours-or-less relationship checkstand.

We are all familiar with the cliché, "There are plenty of fish in the sea." Weber created and legitimized a male cabal who trolled for babes using the catch and release program. This might work for salmon or cod, but not every woman finds it appealing. I have little doubt that the hook, line, and sinker antics of the 1970s led to the Gloria Steinem quip, "A woman needs a man like a fish needs a bicycle."

In short, we blew it.

It wasn't completely our fault. After enduring the sexual repression of the fifties, and braving the unpleasant aftertaste of sixties' free love (i.e., sitar music, communes, and macrobiotic brown rice), the zipless snuggle sounded appealing. Not every guy subscribed to the Weber philosophy, but we would all pay the price. And those who weren't "picking up" were being constantly reminded of this fact by those who were. In 1978, no less a cultural authority than *Mad* magazine released a 45 rpm flexi-disc called "Makin' Out." The chorus proclaimed:

> *Makin' out makin' out*
> *I tell myself I could be, should be makin' out!*
> *But all I'm makin' out, from all this makin' out*
> *Is that everyone's makin' out but me.*

Ignorance can be bliss.

The era of the cheap, paperback advice book ended in the late 1970s, a decline due in large part to the publication of *Jonathan Livingston Seagull*. Yes, books like *Men Who Hate Women and the Women Who Love Them*; *Real Men Don't Eat Quiche;* and *On Your Own* by Brooke Shields were published during the 1980s, but sex advice shifted mediums. Suddenly, bizarre midgets with bad accents (Dr. Ruth) and a computer generated, disembodied version of Matt Frewer (Max Headroom) were explaining condom etiquette. People seemed to prefer watching intelligent moderators like Donahue, Morton Downy Jr., Sally Jesse Raphael, and Geraldo Rivera toss around the important ideas of the day. And the occasional chair.

The most popular advice books in the eighties were about solving Ernö Rubik's irksome invention. Those seeking guidance in matters of the heart had to read between the lines. In *You Can*

Do the Cube, thirteen-year-old schoolboy cubemaster Patrick Bossert slyly suggests, "You may find that your cube is very stiff to turn, in which case you will need to open it up and grease it a bit with some petroleum jelly, such as Vaseline."

When you consider the terrible music (Huey Lewis), the terrible new diseases (AIDS, yuppiedom), and the terrible acting (Steve Guttenberg), the eighties really sucked, despite Jazzercise and Hinkley's attempt to impress Jodie Foster.

Even worse was a new subculture of single men that reveled in their social incompetence. The nerds first stirred with the release of the Apple IIe (1977) and the IBM personal computer (1981), grew stronger with the release of the film *Tron* (1982), and went legit when *Revenge of the Nerds* debuted in 1984.

Normal single guys still suffer the stigmatism of these farsighted overlords. It's the ol' guilty by association rap. If you were an unsuccessful single guy in the 1980s, it was easy to infer that perhaps you were playing too much Dungeons and Dragons or Atari 2600.

Thus began the war against the nerds. Non-nerds had more charisma, wisdom, constitution, and strength, but the pocket-protector people had dexterity, hit points, and enormous bags of gold and silver. The great war didn't conclude until 1993, when *Wired* brokered a cease-fire agreement by making nerd culture socially tolerable and visually appealing (if utterly unreadable). The label of geek was also popularized, allowing for geek chic and other amusing oyxmorons. In exchange for all-you-can-drink Jolt and copious stock options, geeks agreed to hide in their cubicles, patiently waiting for the Internet to ignite.

ISN'T IT IRONIC?
NOT REALLY

In 1989, East Germans finally managed to huff and puff and blow the wall down. The first McDonald's opened in Moscow on January 31, 1990, and communism was no match for such formidable foes as Hamburglar and Grimace. Unfettered capitalism was given the opportunity to prove, once and for all, that greed could soothe the troubled soul as effectively as socialism or chicken soup.

Instead of improving our lives, the invisible hand gave single guys the finger. Certainly, we can buy chunks of the Berlin Wall on eBay, or own a wide-slice toaster that connects to a Local Area Network, or procure the used panties of Japanese schoolgirls from a vending machine, but when it came to providing us with some meaningful way of organizing and understanding our lives, capitalism stunk.

Technological advances fostered isolation, instead of helping to build better communities. Men fractured into a thousand little congregations, worshipping false idols such as *The Simpsons*, *Star Trek: The Next Generation*, and *Buffy, the Vampire Slayer*. The proliferation of niche media (cable television, websites, etc.) meant we could further obsess over our consumer fetish, in lieu of pursuing a meaningful relationship with the opposite sex.

Attempts at providing moral guidance during the 1990s were clumsy. The politically correct movement held some promise and appeal for single guys. Treating women with respect and not saying "nigger" was finally going to be in vogue. Unfortunately, like a Leave-a-Penny, Take-a-Penny tray,

Political Correctness sounded good in theory, but failed in practice. The main problem was that P.C. was poorly executed and stage managed. Antioch College created a set of rules governing the sexual behavior of its students, an edict so ludicrous it was impervious to parody. Speech codes were instituted at some universities. The right jumped all over the left, accusing liberals of suppressing freedom of speech. The academic left retreated into their ivory towers rather than point out the irony of conservative politicians defending the first amendment.

Meanwhile, Christian men throughout North America surprised no one by openly declaring that they were terrible husbands and fathers. Better known as Promise Keepers, they were mostly middle-aged men who claimed to have lost their domestic authority and spiritual purpose, due in large part to employment difficulties. They attempted to establish virtuous manhood through stadium-sized rallies and small discussion groups. It was a return to God and Jesus, and one of the promises of a Promise Keeper is a commitment to practicing spiritual, moral, ethical, and sexual purity. Men were to take responsibility for their actions, and reclaim their spiritual leadership in the household.

The Promise Keepers were lead by Bill McCartney, a former football coach-cum-Christian warrior who tried to battle the secular religion known as consumerism by peddling Promise Keeper hats, mugs, caps, CDs, shirts, and copies of *New Man* magazine. The movement eventually collapsed because of McCartney's lack of business acumen, coupled with the Promise Keeper's inability to effectively confront the social and economic forces that had caused their spiritual breakdown in the first place.

Men's magazines had a bit of a resurgence during the 1990s, as they tried to un-befuddle single guys. But what *Details*, television shows, movies, and celebrity role models offered us amounted to something Susan Faludi, author of *Stiffed: The Betrayal of the American Man*, calls "ornamental culture." As the name implies, ornamental culture is masculinity asserted as an external quality. Cologne became manliness in a can; fashion became an Armani suit of armor to impress fair maidens. The dummy hidden beneath the nice smell and the nice threads was deemed irrelevant.

It didn't have to be like this. *Details* was fairly enjoyable in the early 1990s. Yes, it featured fashion spreads with $250 shirts, but advice columnist Anka Radakovich was a must-read and for a time, *Details* appeared genuinely hip – indie-rock slickster Jon Spencer (of Blues Explosion fame) was even on their payroll. *Details* declined in 1994, when it was revealed that Gen-X Anka was actually thirty-seven and their patina of authenticity soon disappeared. It became apparent that *Details* was trying to profit from our male identity crisis. Their tactics verged on the mathematical: this brand of aftershave + this brand of sunglasses + this brand of jeans + this brand of malt liquor = a modern, urban, upscale man.

I might enjoy drinking copious amounts of Bombay Sapphire to dull the pain, but my hard liquor preference is not a window into my soul. Thinking of personality as some patchwork quilt of competing products yields consumer profiles, instead of fully self-actualized human beings. To summarize *No Logo*, the 400-plus-page anti-marketing screed written by Naomi Klein: "Brands are bad."

If *Details* let us down, the self-help book genre was little better. That 800-pound advice book gorilla, *The Rules: Time Tested Secrets for Capturing the Heart of Mr. Right* did not provide much female elucidation. *The Rules* is the sort of book that often uses *italics* to underscore important ideas for less attentive and/or dim-witted readers. It's similar to *People*'s pioneering use of **bold** to enable their readers to better wade through thickets of dense prose. And oh, what prose it is: "On the first date, avoid staring romantically into his eyes. Otherwise, he will know that you're planning the honeymoon."

I realize I'm the 7,849th pundit to mock this book, so I'll now kink my garden hose of vitriol. There is a more important reason I'm uncomfortable quibbling about *The Rules*. After reading *How to Pick Up Girls!,* I realized they're the same book. Both sold millions of copies. Both were designed to achieve a specific purpose, with the end justifying the means. Both provide very clear, simple advice. *The Rules* explains how to get married; *Girls* explains how to get laid.

Both books are sexually regressive. (*The Rules* features advice such as, "Men like women who are neat and clean. They also make better mothers of their children – the kind who don't lose their kids at the beach.") But they deliver on their respective promises. The fact that *The Rules* explains how to get a husband and *Girls!* explains how to finesse some meaningless sex, illustrates the fundamental disconnect between guys and dolls.

In many ways, single men have never had it better, and never had it worse. Francis Fukuyama suggested that the nineties ushered in the end of history. We are post-everything (consumer, punk, religion) and have the ability to reinvent ourselves constantly. Unfortunately, many of us suffer from option paralysis.

And so, I would like to officially point the finger at postmodernism for the single guy predicament. In the 1950s, we had too many rules. Now we have none.

Before you start thinking I'm a Christian fundamentalist who spends most of his time in his basement, trying to construct a Way-Bac machine, let me assure you otherwise. I realize the fifties were filled with terrible things like bigotry, sexism, and Maynard G. Krebs.

What I like is the *idea* of the fifties, not the specifics. The fifties still retains the aura of a nation slowly discovering its sexuality. Despite all the negatives, you have to admit, with all those tight sweaters and cantilevered bras, the fifties PR department did an amazing job. It was a naïve, fun, and foolish adventure, as North America coyly groped about, hoping to cop a feel.

There is nothing mysterious about love and sex in the twenty-first century. Pornography has become mainstream. We all know what a money shot is, even if we pretend otherwise. We recognize the names Ron Jeremy, Traci Lords, and Nina Hartley. We've seen *Boogie Nights*. And the Internet makes viewing barely legal teens, anytime, anywhere, an effortless exercise. Never again will single guys have to deal with the shame of the Back Door of the Video Store – an embarrassment barricade that saved us from ourselves. The triple-w means every quirk you can fathom (yes, even situations involving donkeys and grandmothers) is a click away. There is something to be said for intrigue. Stag films featured blurry, fleeting images, and dirty postcards were laughably tame. In *A Stiff Drink and a Close Shave*, authors Bob Sloan and Steven Guarnaccia point out the playfulness of Girlie images. Buxom, leggy, and *décolletage*, these shapely, seductive sketches were obviously make-believe, affirming that men were libidinous, lecherous, leering fools.

Planet Pornography is bizarro world, the Very Lonely Planet's *doppelgänger* – a silicon Wonderland where women sequentially shed their sheer outer garments and lacy undergarments at the mere sight of a camera lens or klieg light. Men and women move through this land like pieces on a board game, playing a more adult version of Clue – *it was Mrs. Peacock, in the bedroom, with the whip.*

This propaganda is obviously false, filled as it is with couples who are constantly engaged in impossible feats – like baby making – while displaying the acrobatic pyrotechnics of circus contortionists. Despite these scenarios being as choreographed as professional wrestling and as fake as the first moon landing, many single guys are convinced a world like this really exists.

These ribald images divert us from our girlfriend quest and veer us towards a collision course with Fantasy Island, where "da plane" is filled with soon-to-be off-duty stewardesses, including a pair of twin sisters and a set of triplets. The sad thing is that the deception is so complete and pervasive that finding the clarity of mind to ignore all the cleavage and the pouting lips and the firm, fleshy curves of the young women that glisten under diffused lighting may well be impossible.

I realize that despite my impassioned pleas, pornography isn't going to disappear – it's a multi-billion dollar industry. It continues to capture our attention and imagination – both ordinary guy Ian Brown (author of *Man Overboard*, an exploration of modern masculinity) and feminist Susan Faludi spent time on porn film sets under the guise of research.

Porn is mental cholesterol. It slowly clogs your imagination, replacing healthy fantasies of your own creation with triple-X plaque. The insert tab A into slot B routine takes on a depressing monotony, like watching a toy Drinking Happy Bird bob its head, take a sip of water, and then repeat the process ad infinitum. A relationship, however rare, is always in 3-D. A porn actress will always be decidedly two-dimensional.

Newton theorized that every action has an opposite and equal reaction. Relegating 1950s social etiquette to the dustbin of history has hidden costs. Without the reassuring warmth of the Cold War, we have lost both the threat of mutually assured destruction and the potential for furtive, "fifteen minutes before the bomb drops" panic sex.

Postmodernism has stripped away any semblance of an understandable or sane world. The lack of rules has created a lot of romantic casualties, not to mention a new, imprecise language. Words like boyfriend and girlfriend have been replaced with doublespeak that would confuse even O'Brien.

In the 1950s, everything was black and white. If you wanted to sculpt your hair, you used Brylcreem. There was no gel, mousse, molder, spritz, defrizzer, shaper, styler, or hair cement. And if you had something to say, you said it. You took no guff. There was a rich vernacular:

» insouciance
» peccadilloes
» addlepated
» moral turpitude
» chaperone

» licentious
» vodka-sodden rake
» "park"ing and "spark"ing
» mashers
» sweater girl in the typing pool
» deep-freeze act
» bad stork scares
» being caught in flagrante delecto
» venereal disease
» paramour
» gams
» malarkey
» rum-bucket
» trollop, hussy, tart, shrew, deb
» haberdashery

No one says what they really mean anymore. Higher education is partly to blame. In university, I was taught that using two paragraphs to state something as simple as "there are seven days in a week" is completely reasonable:

When looking at chronological inventory there are many things to consider, including the weekend, the role of Mondays in a social context (Garfield, et al.), and the pagan rituals associated with the arrival of Fridays. As well, it is important to note that there is still much research needed on the conventions and misunderstandings surrounding the phrase "the day before yesterday."

Finally, considerations must be given to the role of the Julian and Gregorian calendars in the historical development of the week as we know it (Al, et al.). However, be that as it may, few modern scholars would disagree with a paradigmatic structure incorporating the sentiment that there are seven days in a week.

It is said that the Inuit have twenty-five words to describe snow (white, wet, white *and* wet, yellow, etc.). Similarly, our pomo lexicon has grown over the years to give us a nearly unlimited ability to articulate our relationship limbos:

> » We're seeing each other
> » We're seeing parts of each other
> » We're having outercourse
> » We're not exclusive
> » We're in the nine items or less checkout
> » This is my partner
> » This is my significant other
> » This is my lady friend
> » This is a two-week relationship (TWR) with renewal possibilities
> » We're leasing with an option to buy
> » I'm involved
> » I'm a serial monogamist
> » We're living in sin
> » We're seeing what happens during this red light

But where has it gotten us? In his essay "Politics and the English Language," respected dead English author George Orwell explained that language, "becomes ugly and inaccurate because our thoughts are foolish, but the slovenliness of our language makes it easier for us to have foolish thoughts." Orwell identified the problem back in 1946, well before phrases such as "ethnic cleansing" and "Christian scientist" existed. He foresaw that convoluted descriptions of romantic entanglements were doubleplus ungood.

Vague words and phrases have created a lot of unhappiness. Our first instinct, upon meeting that special someone, should be to grab a pen and write a perfume-scented mash note. Instead, we reach for a thesaurus to figure out how to best play euphemism euthanasia.

Back in the fifties, things were different. If you carved both your initials into a tree, it was love. If you carried her books home from school, it was love. If a girl wore an over-sized sweater, or had a ring on her necklace, it meant she had a boyfriend. And if a girl got pregnant, it meant the boy was grounded for life and the girl had to go live with her aunt in a nearby town.

It is worth noting that not one, but two retro-revivals occurred during the nineties. While the resurrection of Swing was nifty, I have two left feet. I also have problems with a trend jump-started by a Gap commercial. I was more enthralled with the Cocktail Nation that emerged in early 1994.

When I lived in Vancouver, the Niagara – a badly-lit beer trough – hosed down the filth every Wednesday, unfolded some tablecloths, lit some candles, and transformed itself into something called Gin 'n' Sin. Men wore suits (in fact, you were turned away at the door if you weren't in appropriate attire) and women wore evening dresses and/or kimonos.

The night previous, these same patrons had been chug-ging cheap draft, clothed in torn jeans and black t-shirts. Transformed by gowns and suits that hid their tattoos, these grunge mavens became lounge lizards – happily imbibing martinis as they listened to Esquivel, Martin Denny, Julie London, and the Rat Pack.

Because Lounge was able to incorporate a wider swatch of contradictions, it was more punk rock and iconoclastic than Swing. Sid Vicious, did, after all, do a cover of "My Way." Swing told you how to dress and how to dance while Lounge kids tried to irritate their parents by emulating them.

According to the "First Manifesto of the Cocktail Nation" written by The Millionaire from the band Combustible Edison: "We pledge to revolt against the void of dictated sobriety and to cultivate not riches but richness, swankness, suaveness and strangeness, with pleasure and boldness for all. BE FABULOUS."

Naugahyde might appear ahistorical, but the repressed desires of fifties society were addressed, to varying degrees of success, in the cocktail lounge. By day, the guy in the grey flannel suit battled communism and Bernie in Accounts Receivable. At night, resplendent in a Hawaiian shirt, stoked by mood music and cloaked in atmospheric lighting, he could temporarily let his guard down.

The 1990s Cocktail Nation was partly a reaction against the depressing lack of sartorial savvy displayed by the flannel folk of the Seattle scene. Lounge wasn't perfect, and it grappled with issues of camp and kitsch and irony and the celebration of inauthenticity. Hedonism was nifty, but fezzes and gabardine and soap bubble machines and Pink Ladies weren't quite as revolutionary as The Millionaire made them out to be when he announced, "We, the Citizens of the Cocktail Nation, do hereby declare our independence from the desiccated horde of mummified uniformity – our freedom from an existence of abject swinglessness."

My favorite Lounge song was a regressive little ditty by Robert Mitchum (Max Cady in the original *Cape Fear*) called "Not Me." It's from his *Calypso Is Like So . . .* album. The chorus went:

It is the people who say
that the men are leading the women astray.
But I say that the women of today
are smarter than men in every way.

A vigorous defense of this song will create a kind of feminist finger trap I'd prefer to avoid. When Mitchum chants, "the women play the men like a puppet show," I know he's wrong, but who cares? Gin 'n' Sin offered an oasis from "isms" and other bothersome, thought-provoking ideologies that made guys feel guilty about glancing at the cigarette girl. Lounge was a safe, booze-filled biosphere with rituals and clearly defined gender roles. You were allowed to ask a woman to dance, and not feel like a creep, because you actually wanted to dance with her. The lounge subculture provided a social framework for men who were not comfortable with traditional beer commercial bars and the meatmarket therein. Best of all, the music was played at a volume that allowed for conversation.

At the end of the night, as you stumbled out the doors of the Niagara, the fantasy gently evaporated. You woke up the next morning and groggily toiled away in a cubicle orchard, or nodded off in a university lecture hall. But for a few hours the night previous, you felt you understood how the world worked.

The cocktail nation conquered from 1994 until 1996. Either it was ruined by mainstream media attention, or it simply ran its course. It was an interesting experiment. It provided a quick peek at what once was. It combined the advantages and benefits of the modern world, with a controlled return to the past – a kind of historical smorgasbord. Mourn its death the next time you're quaffing Bud at a sports bar filled with brass and ferns.

THE BUSINESS OF PLEASURE

Despite Castro's best efforts, capitalism dominated the ideological Olympics of the nineties. The main result of the free market triumph was that business-speak became the dominant slang. If advertisers treat men and women like consumers, not citizens, being an unproductive, costly romantic fool might not be the best way to succeed. Perhaps we guys should abandon all pretense of love and discuss matters in actuarial terms.

Men will no longer be dumped, but downsized.

We're no longer single, either. As Melissa Banks notes in *Girl's Guide to Hunting and Fishing*, a singles event connotes individually wrapped American cheese slices. I would instead like to popularize the phrase "between relationships," which implies previous and future dalliances with some measure of confidence. Men who are "between relationships" are "free agents" working diligently in the mergers and acquisitions sector.

The government needs to declare dates tax deductible. We require some motivational, single guy-themed Successories. We might even have to do the unthinkable and follow the asinine advice of business guru Tom Peters. In August 1997 he wrote an infamous article for *Fast Company* entitled, "The Brand Called You." In it, he suggests we are all CEOs of Me Inc. Or, to put it another way: "Brands are good."

Many people have savaged this article, including Naomi Klein, the aforementioned author of the 400-plus-page anti-marketing screed *No Logo*. "Tom Peters," she argues, "is bad."

As frightening as the thought of a personal brand extension might be, it's already happening. In a March 20, 1997 article entitled "Single White Product," the editors of FeedMag.com paid for reporter Steve Bodow to have a personal focus group assess his dating potential.

Single guys are the RC Cola of the gene pool. We're as effervescent as other men, but we lack a good logo and a catchy slogan. For two hours, Bodow sat behind the two-way mirror and endured nine women picking apart his CV and analyzing various photos. They observed:

> » "He's not bad looking, but he doesn't, you know, send chills down my spine or anything."
> » "He's definitely more Heineken than Budweiser."
> » "He seems manic-depressive to me."

So what did Bodow learn from the experience? In matters appearance-related, he decided to ditch a cheap suit purchased at Moe Ginsburg. As for helping Bodow reposition his personality, he felt the process had severe limitations. The fact that he was both bohemian (dabbling in theatre and freelance writing) and business-like (a stint as an investment analyst) irritated the focus group. They wanted Bodow to adopt a clear direction – a unique sales proposition – instead of drifting through life. Unfortunately, this suggestion is better suited to celebrities, not ordinary guys. According to Bodow, the format of all focus groups is designed to elicit such a response, compressing "complicated personalities into neat comprehensible caricatures."

The focus group route might not be the perfect solution. I'm not sure I need a bunch of strange women telling me to be less Pillsbury Doughboy and more Mr. Peanut. Still, there's no arguing that the "neat, comprehensible caricature" route has worked depressingly well in the democratic arena. Perhaps, like a good politician, you should leave the voter (your date) with a maximum of two or three themes or slogans. In the CBC television show *The Newsroom*, George Findlay (Ken Finkleman), a news director-cum-campaign manager, counsels news anchor-cum-political candidate Jim Walcott (Peter Keleghan). "Don't discuss any complicated issues. Just say 'Cut the deficit, create jobs.'"

Steve Bodow believes that "everyone wants a smart guy with a good sense of humor, sensitive but not wimpy." If you're funny, deliver one great joke instead of six adequate ones. If you're smart, limit your intellectual acrobatics to one topic. And a lone barroom brawl should prove your aversion to quiche.

Women claim they like complex men – e.g., the nuanced acting of Keanu Reeves – but you don't want to spend your first date baffling her. Successive dates can return to and expand upon your original themes and strengths, helping to explain why a corporate merger is in the woman's best interest. Don't hesitate to utilize brightly-colored bar graphs or pie charts.

The business metaphor is also useful when it comes to a dating Catch-22 – single women are often interested in guys who are already in a relationship. The reasoning (so far as I can tell) is that if a guy is taken, he must have something worth having. To put it another way, few people rent an empty apartment.

This tendency reminds me of corporate headhunters who try to woo you away from your current metier. They'll ask things like, "Are you happy with your current job?"

Also consider this: How do you get a job/girlfriend? Experience.

How do you get experience?

Get a job/girlfriend.

This sell-short technique is helpful to no one. If men are a commodity, then I urge women to approach single guys with a buy-low, sell-high mentality. Yes, we're romantically dyslexic, but we can be trained to use the correct fork when eating salad and to not slurp soup. We just need some tricks and tips to ensure we don't reverse our "ds" and "bs" or invert our "ms" and "ws."

Do you want the shiny red Testarosa or a dull grey Volvo? Women need to realize we're masculine mutual funds – over the long term she'll be pleasantly surprised by our rate of return.

Being friends with a woman also fits within the contours of the business metaphor. Getting chummy with a gal is the equivalent of interning for a corporation you'd really, really, really like to work for. After volunteering for a few months, the boss will probably enjoy the work you're doing, but has no intention of ever paying you.

A better route is to fill out an application form, and ensure Human Resources keeps your résumé on file. Call back every few months to see if a position needs to be filled, but apply for other jobs. Your initiative and confidence may well impress your future boss.

For the past ten years or so, Bart Ellis, a Los Angeles social worker and relationship expert, has offered to improve dating skills – for a price. His Date Doctor service allows you to spend a few hours with an actor/paramour who provides a relationship report card on the satisfactory and needs improvement aspects of your seduction schtick. Brutally honest, (bad breath, boring), it gives you an opportunity to eradicate or obfuscate negative traits, thereby improving your marketability.

A final thought: given the litigious nature of the victim-mentality-prone United States, a country where people receive money for spilling hot coffee on themselves, why blame yourself? Sue your date for the emotional distress of being rejected.

When it comes to the actual date, the best analog is the world of politics. The most apt metaphor for dating in the new millennium is the televised debate. Well-meaning friends are spin doctors, suggesting platform planks ("I like children, animals, and the elderly"), providing image consultancy ("Choose a dimly lit restaurant"), and identifying the weaknesses of your opponent ("She can't hold her liquor"). According to American folklore, radio listeners thought Nixon had out-debated JFK in 1960. But Nixon's refusal to use makeup, coupled with his five-o'clock shadow, convinced television viewers he was evil incarnate.

Politicians no longer attempt dramatic debating victories; they focus instead on avoiding mistakes. Lloyd Bentsen drubbing Dan Quayle in the 1988 Vice-presidential debate with "Senator, you are no Jack Kennedy" is now part of the pop culture pantheon. That sort of gaffe hasn't occurred since. I have every confidence I will one day end a date with a Reaganesque, "Are you better off now than you were four hours ago?"

Both debates and dates are about presenting the best,

most tightly scripted, odorless version of yourself. Men are expected to be "on." Single guys will never, ever admit this, but we prepare for dates ahead of time – and I don't mean the fresh underwear and shaving routine. We rehearse a (hopefully) humorous anecdote or two, we researh the current crop of date movies (selecting an appropriate film is crucial, as *Taxi Driver* taught us), and we put her name into Google.com.

Improved search engine algorithms allow guys to discover useless information about the woman they fancy. The only problem is ensuring your date doesn't discover you e-vetted them. Mentioning an obscure fact about her will make you sound like a character in a badly written mystery novel.

Despite all this courtship homework, spontaneity eventually intercedes. As a political commentator noted long ago, human nature means that no matter what kind of script is drilled into our heads, after about ninety minutes, we're bound to drift and start acting like a human being, or worse, ourselves. Do your best to avoid a relationship-killing blunder.

Finally, I'd like to encourage exit polling. When a woman says no way, we generally aren't told exactly why. Single guys are pure trial and error, never discovering the patterns that help or hinder them. (There's a reason it's called "getting lucky.") We need to know if we were close or not even. Toward this end, it would really be helpful if women filled out a "How did I do today"-style survey.

Scream has the honor of being the first postmodern slasher flick (i.e., a character named Randy mocks the genre by noting, "There are certain rules you must abide by in order to successfully survive a horror movie"). Adapting this format only slightly, it appears our society is primed for the terror of postmodern dating. I realize I criticized postmodernism earlier, but perhaps the cause of our problems might also solve them. How very – well – postmodern.

If we know how the enemy is supposed to be thinking, why not openly acknowledge it? I would truly enjoy a dinner date featuring a play-by-play commentator sitting at the table – a pomo chaperone assessing my chances, offering advice, and cracking a few jokes. We could even have a commercial break every seven minutes.

Lest you think I'm crazy, those wily Japanese have developed something called the Future Diary service at the Korakuen amusement park in Tokyo. Future Diary is basically a scripted date – couples receive their own instruction book! – designed to create a memorable evening. Paid actors even interact with the couple – in one scenario, the lovebirds must help a lost foreign child.

I find this idea quite appealing. And since most single guy encounters are unintentionally funny, why not push it one notch further and create a Sitcom Date:

> She: I'll go on a date with you, but first you must spend the night in my crazy Uncle Slotvik's haunted mansion.
> You: Will you keep me company?
> She: No.
> You: Can I bring some Scooby snacks?
> [laugh track swells]

The free market provides solutions, but at a price. Unfortunately, romantic charity is far less sophisticated. I tried organizing a bachelor auction once, but it quickly turned into the silent variety. Still, I've founded two non-profit organizations. The first is called the Make-A-Reasonable-Wish Foundation (MARW).

The MARW Foundation grants the requests of single men with life-threatening loneliness to enrich the human experience with hope, strength, and comely celebrities. The Foundation becomes aware of a man's desire through wish referrals, which are accepted from friends, family, therapists, and ex-girlfriends. Last year, MARW helped twelve long-suffering men shake hands with and eat lunch at an "appropriate distance" from actresses such as Mira Sorvino, Angelina Jolie, and Reese Witherspoon.

The second charity case is Save-the-Single-Guy. In the roughest synapses of the Very Lonely Planet are hobos of concupiscence who need your help. I urge you to consider sponsoring a single guy.

Save-the-Single-Guy

Right now, sitting on a dirty street corner in Kansas is a lonely guy. He might be drunk—we're not sure—but we can confirm his loneliness. He is begging for sexual favors with a cardboard sign.

Right now, in a kitchen in Halifax, John is pouring himself a cup of coffee and sitting down to read the morning paper. His tears are so copious that even the headline is obscured.

Right now, she is going on with her life.

For just forty-three cents a day, you can bring a little joy into a single man's life by giving him the ability to purchase a tattered photocopy of a naked Alyssa Milano.

Your sponsorship will allow single men access to clean water (Evian), good food (Tiramisu), and low grade titillation. Your financial support also provides single guys with hope for a better future and the knowledge that someone cares about them. This gift is priceless.

If you're a woman, consider giving a less fortunate man a kiss. It need only be on the cheek, but it'll be a start to boosting his confidence and making the world a better place.

Thank you, and God bless.

Help us help them.

Save-the-Single-Guy

MONO-SAPIEN

single guys in profile

XY CHEMISTRY 101

The single guy possesses the unique ability to be self-reflective about his masculinity. We think about thinking about being men. This gift is often taken to tragic extremes, and the guy in question spends most of his mental horse-power developing reasons *not* to ask out a woman. Descartes dubbed this phenomenon *Cogito, cogito ergo sum nada* (I think too much, therefore I am alone).

It's a shame some men get punished for attempting to create a nuanced version of masculinity, because balancing raw emotion with deep thought is a noble goal. It isn't easy being an Astute Brute.

What, exactly, is an Astute Brute? He's a dynamic individual, constantly negotiating and renegotiating exactly where he sits, or doesn't sit, on the spectrum of manliness. He questions media constructions of masculinity. He is pro-choice. He is comfortable, but not too comfortable with his femininity. He's heard of, and perhaps even skimmed through, the SCUM Manifesto. He became blubbery during the final minutes of *The English Patient*. He is able to recognize when mistakes have been made. He is capable of genuine and sustained levels of guilt regarding past actions. He's the guy who really does read *Playboy* for the articles.

Moose, of *Archie* comics fame, is not an Astute Brute. He is all brute; the kind of guy who never stops to think about brain-busting concepts such as male gaze or patriarchal hegemony.

Noam Chomsky is also not an Astute Brute. He is too astute; the sort of fellow who has never, ever, changed a flat tire or yearned to shout "Shower!" at a strip club.

Astute Brute archetypes exist, if you know where to look. The most recent and thus best example, is the 1996 film *Swingers*, which traces the exploits of Mike Peters (Jon Favreau), a guy who has moved to L.A., from New York. His girlfriend of six years, who remains in New York, has just left him. His Lothario buddy Trent Walker (Vince Vaughn), tries to shake Mike out of his funk.

Swingers acts as a serviceable docudrama about the habitat and habits of the single guy, given Mike's depressing apartment and pathetic mannerisms (he spends a considerable part of each day drinking orange juice and feeling sorry for himself).

Mike is unrelenting solipsism, while Trent's advice for approaching women is pure alpha male: men are big bears with claws and fangs, women are little bunnies cowering in the corner. Mike finds a new love interest only when he strikes a judicious balance between Astute and Brute. Trent's bear/bunny dichotomy gives Mike the confidence to approach Lorraine (Heather Graham) at a bar, but as soon as he starts talking to her, he treats her like a person, instead of feeding her lines. Unfortunately, most single guys require more than ninety minutes to figure out how to balance these two elements successfully.

Leslie Fiedler's *Love and Death in the American Novel* coined the term Good Bad Boy. Best embodied by Huck Finn, he is "America's vision of itself, crude and unruly in his beginnings but endowed by his creator with an instinctive sense of what is right." This is the ideal goal of an Astute Brute. The Bad Boy is pure Brute, a state of being we'll never achieve by virtue of the speedbump known as our brain, and the Good Boy often finishes last. But there is no reason we can't flavor

79

our lives with some masculine MSG. We need to act first and ask questions later, instead of thinking first and acting much, much later, if at all.

Because the Astute Brute is inherently complex (if not confused), creating a character sketch of the typical AB is difficult. But just as Canadians define themselves as not being American, it will be convenient to define the Astute Brute by what he isn't. He isn't homophobic. He hates AC/DC and Aerosmith and enjoys bands with weirdo names like Death Cab for Cutie and Guided by Voices. He isn't obsessed with professional sports. He doesn't obsess about his abs. He doesn't lift heavy objects for a living, instead utilizing his brain in fields such as graphic design, journalism, or middle-management. He has never judged a wet t-shirt contest. He thinks violence against women is bad. He finds anorexia unsexy and if he had a girlfriend, he definitely wouldn't think she looks fat. He thinks one-night stands are passé (although envy tempers his opinion). He has never donned a hardhat and catcalled at female pedestrians. He has a low Degree of Dolphin Affinity (DoDA). The odor of potpourri makes him nauseous. He doesn't understand a word Oprah is saying. He thinks breast implants are disgusting, ever since he saw *The Girl Next Door*, a documentary about porn actress Stacy Valentine. The footage of her augmentation surgery was so painful to watch that he would not wish it on his worst enemy.

Finally, the Astute Brute hates *Maxim* magazine.

Now, I don't want to go off on a tirade here, but *Maxim* is clearly the root of all evil. It may be wrong to blame a bunch of perfect-bound, glossy pages for the downfall of society, but

Maxim is the lowest common denominator of the lowest common denominator. I know women who have read *Maxim* to gain trenchant insight about men, only to learn that we are driven by six things: sex, sports, beer, gadgets, clothes, fitness. This is analogous to a man reading *Cosmo* so he can figure out what Gloria Steinem is thinking.

Maxim offers men an opportunity to get in touch with their "inner swine" and allows them to mentally revert back to junior high. The average *Maxim* reader is thirty. *Advertising Age* dubbed this demographic "adultescents." I'd call it "pathetic."

I suppose not everyone *has* to read *The New Yorker*, or *Harper's,* or *The Baffler*, or *McSweeneys*, or *The Onion*, or *Punk Planet,* or *Bust*, or *Hermenaut,* or the many other *Magazines Featuring Ideas Instead of Nearly Naked Women*. But the frustrating thing about *Maxim* is that prior to its emergence, men simply weren't buying general interest magazines.

So what's better: nothing, or *Maxim?* In the fifties and sixties, when *Playboy* ruled manland, it featured interviews with heavyweights like Martin Luther King Jr. and Marshall McLuhan, and fiction by Kurt Vonnegut Jr. and Roald Dahl. *Maxim*'s investigative journalism begins and ends with pee-shy guys.

Reading *Maxim* is the equivalent of going to Europe for two weeks and spending ninety percent of the vacation watching television in your hotel room and making the occasional safari to McDonald's. No one can deny that you've been to Europe, but everyone will cast dispersions on the quality of your trip. Granted, not every guy wants to come home from a hard day at work and puzzle through an article entitled "Transgressing the Boundaries: Towards a Transformative Hermeneutics of Quantum Gravity." The guilty pleasure has an honorable tradition in our society.

What plays havoc with my synapses is the regressive formula *Maxim* utilizes. In *The Hidden Persuaders,* crusading journalist Vance Packard analyzes *True* (the Man's Magazine). During the fifties, *True* had a circulation of two million, utilizing a combination of male reassurance and female repression. It featured stories about boxing and prostitution and car racing and Bigfoot and the military. I have a copy of *Cartoon Laffs from True,* a compilation of doodles and *bon mots* from the magazine, circa 1958. It features jokes about buxom blondes, newlyweds, alcoholics, trophy secretaries, women drivers, and killing your wife.

As Packard noted, *True* treated its readers as if "they were all hairy-chested sourdoughs who had just returned from a tramp in the woods." Speaking in 1956, *True* editorial director Ralph Daigh attributed the success of *True* to the fact that it "stimulates masculine ego at a time when men want to fight back against women's efforts to usurp his traditional role as head of the family." Sound familiar? In 1999, *Maxim*'s circulation was a little over two million. Not much has changed in over forty years. We've come a very short way, baby. As men, we can do better. There is nothing Astute about *Maxim.*

The worst thing about Maxim is how it has forced other men's magazines to dumb down. This might suprise you, but *National Geographic* didn't always have a swimsuit issue.

My Astute Brute concept isn't the first attempt at balancing brain and brawn. What is hopefully new about my male genus is that it allows for mixtures of the two elements. This provides for a more complex, rounded kind of man. Convincing women such a guy exists might be difficult, however, since the sins of the frat-boy have been visited upon the single guy for many generations.

It is important to remember that the Astute and the Brute have limits, as illustrated by the Chomsky and Moose examples. The trick is finding a pleasant equilibrium. A guy who decides to be a bit Brute should consider the cautious pig approach. This involves finding a clever way of being salacious – "She's friends with Russ Meyer" – instead of simply saying "Nice rack." Think of it as locker-room talk lite – Now With Thirty Percent Less Boorishness!

The fact that the Astute Brute isn't P.C.-perfect doesn't make him immediately condemnable. No man is without fault, but the Astute Brute concept acknowledges that our numerous imperfections are continually being identified and rectified.

I draw inspiration for the Astute Brute concept from *Fight Club* (both the 1999 film, and the 1997 novel by Chuck Palahniuk). If you haven't read or seen either, I'm about to ruin them, so either skip the next five paragraphs, or censor yourself by only reading every third word.

Fight Club pushes the identity crisis of North American males to its logical conclusion. The difference between worker drone and consumer stooge Jack (Joe in the novel) and anarchistic, tough-guy Tyler Durden is a perfect cleave between the poles of Astute and Brute. In the novel, Joe notes, "Tyler is funny and charming and forceful and independent, and men look up to him and expect him to change their world. Tyler is capable and free, and I am not."

Near the end of *Fight Club*, it's revealed that Tyler and Joe are the same person ("We both use the same body, but at different times"), although the Astute Joe and the Brute Tyler keep their actions completely separate. While Joe "sleeps," Tyler does his dirty work: he sets up underground boxing leagues in cities throughout America and later creates a male militia that engineers culture jamming-style pranks under the rubric Project Mayhem.

Fight Club is big, bold, loud, and lacking in subtlety. But it touches on some very relevant issues. In the film, Tyler harangues a gathering by noting, "Advertising has us chasing cars and clothes, working jobs we hate so we can buy shit we don't need."

The cathartic release of watching ordinary guys pound the bejeesus out of each other requires no further analysis. Tyler, however, adds an extra layer of complexity by creating a set of clearly defined rules that govern both the fisticuffs and Project Mayhem. In fact, if you want to get spooky, there are seven rules of Fight Club and seven promises of the Promise Keepers.

Like the confused, middle-aged males that formed the Promise Keepers, the twenty-something men in Project Mayhem so desperately crave order and purpose that they're willing to worship a madman to assuage their existential vacuum. *Fight Club* suggests there are a lot of men who feel like flotsam in the sea of postmodernism, and anyone who offers to redirect the tidal patterns will be as revered as Poseidon.

Here is where things get complicated. All single guys are Astute Brutes. But the amount of testosterone and the ability to analyze it varies. Think of Astute and Brute as volatile chemical compounds – small fluctuations in concentration create very different pH levels. Here then is a periodic table of single guys (see Fig. 1). Like atomic elements, certain personality quirks can be combined to create very big loser molecules.

Nerd

The Nerd finds the precision of technology far more appealing than the uncertainty of social interaction. Thus, his Bruteness atrophies, and with it, his ability to interface with females. Yet the nerd nearly achieved alpha male status in the late nineties, as IPO billionaires and Internet executives littered the covers of *Business 2.0*. Linus Torvalds was elevated to hero status for the liberating powers of Linux and Shawn Fanning became a virtual rock star for liberating the music of real-life rock stars. Unfortunately, despite James Bond-worthy gadgets (Palm Pilots) and uninhibited pagan festivals (Burning Man), nerds were unable to augment their Brute or debug their love lives. When the e-revolution promised by e-tailers like StypticPencils.com failed to materialize, their fifteen minutes of nerd fame went 404, and with it, their chances with the opposite sex.

Peter Pandemic

Some single guys have trouble adapting to the big, bad, scary world of adulthood. Whether this means owning a single bed (the worst kind of self-fulfilling prophecy) or having a king-sized bed with a dinosaur-patterned duvet, or living with your parents, too much inner boy means too little girl-related joy.

Dull Man

What's the difference between boring and dull? According to DullMen.com, boring men toil under the delusion that they are interesting; an extroverted dull guy is a boring guy. Dull Men accept their designation and live satisfying, introverted lives. They enjoy zwieback and marmite, and for kicks they boil water or watch wet paint turn arid. There are more ho-hum men than you might think – the book *Boring Postcards* is in its second printing, and there's even a *Journal of Mundane Behavior* (MundaneBehavior.org). Dull Men are reliable to a fault, but thrill-seeking women often shack up with MacGyvers, and pay for their decision with divorce and heart-break. The solution seems painfully obvious: find a dull woman. Nuh-uh. According to DullMen.com, "Women are not dull. Women are exciting."

Romantic Klutz

The kind of guy that is photo-finish close to not being single, but always manages to get a seemingly insignificant dating detail wrong. Like the castaways on Gilligan's Island, every time it appears escape is imminent, something spoils the deal – usually a coconut or a sliver of bamboo. Take my advice, that spaghetti scene from *Lady and the Tramp* does not work with dry pasta. Nor does surprising your date by answering the front door wearing nothing but Saran Wrap.

Nice Guy, a.k.a. Sensitive Guy

The Nice Guy is, we are told, the most in-demand kind of male. And contrary to popular belief, we're not all married, gay, dead, or serving time for crimes we didn't commit. There are plenty of nice guys out there, but we're difficult to spot. Just as some people are color blind or tone deaf, nice guys are flirting-challenged. When forced to discern friendly from frisky behavior, they too often err on the side of caution. They refuse to believe that prolonged eye contact, the famed "hair toss," or a vigorous soul kiss have prurient motives. Unfortunately, there is a very fine line between acting coy and being clue-less. By consistently mistaking positive reinforcement as neutral stimuli, Nice Guys perpetuate their own extinction myth.

Very Hopeless Romantic

Some of us have a problem shifting from lala-land to reality: we daydream constantly about Planet Romance, a mythical place steeped in the warm hues of Kodachrome, where couples wash their car, occasionally squirting each other, as they laugh and love. Such images loop endlessly through the mind of the Very Hopeless Romantic; a less gory version of the Zapruder film.

Placing your jacket over a mud puddle or soaking your girlfriend with a garden hose are appealing prospects, but having your head in the clouds means your feet rarely touch the pavement. The Very Hopeless Romantic has less trouble than most single guys in attracting women, but he harbors unrealistic relationship expectations. As soon as some heavy emotional lifting is required, he panics and retreats.

Self-Esteem Hobo

Single guys watch women flock to prettyboys with room temperature IQs and conclude that only plastic surgery can solve their problems. They are unable to appreciate the importance of confidence. Low self-esteem prevents the Hobo from realizing that more than a few women might actually want to go out with him.

Checklist Boy

Many single guys, especially those unattached for more than a year, begin to upgrade, rather than downgrade, their expectations for a mate. This might seem stupid, but after hunting for so long, it makes some sense to wait a bit longer to find the perfect girlfriend. If you've been single for two years, waiting an extra two months is negligible. Love is not a laundry list, however, and some single guys want five-girlfriends-in-one to make up for lost time. Instead of battling the Madonna/whore complex (a problem, might I interject, that was solved in the personage of Ms. Ciccone), Checklist Boy is looking for Sybil. This type of guy needs to learn the art of comprise – he must become supple like a willow that bends without breaking. Maintaining high standards is worthwhile, but you don't need to be as ramrod as rebar.

Rube Goldberg Syndrome

Instead of pursuing the shortest route between two points – asking a woman for coffee – single guys have a tendency to concoct convoluted dating procedures. Since many single guys are shy, they try to overcome this handicap by attempting everything but the most effective or obvious solution – being less shy. To paraphrase dead English politician Winston Churchill, "A single guy will do the right thing after exhausting every other option."

In February of 2000, I interviewed Conrad Martin, a fifty-year-old divorcée, carpeting consultant, inventor, and entrepreneur. He was a very amicable, normal, sane fellow who had created a brand new hand gesture (and accompanying website – SingleFriendly.com) to help single guys. Formed by crossing the index and middle finger (in a manner strikingly similar to crossing one's fingers for good luck) the single signal means, "See you tomorrow at the same time at the same place."

The single signal seems like a great idea, but when you start wrestling with the logistical quandaries, you quickly drift into the noble failure department. For example, what if the signaled person is interested, but isn't available to meet you the following day at the same time at the same place? "That would be a problem," Martin said. "If it was really someone I wanted to meet, I would try showing up the next day, and the day after that."

Achilles Jr.

An otherwise great guy ruined beyond redemption by a lone personality trait (being a poor listener) or physical feature (having a goatee). What makes this problem so wrenching is that single guys are usually Astute enough to identify their encumbrances, but like that spot in the middle of your back you can never scratch, a tiny, fatal flaw remains beyond our grasp. In most cases, the idiosyncracy can be reversed, but it requires unheralded bravery from the friend of an Achilles Jr., who finally tells him the ugly truth.

Accidental Misogynist

The longer a guy is single, the easier it is to blame the female of the species for his lack of gender relations. The Accidental Misogynist repels hausfraus because his ideas and actions function as a signpost that reads "No Gurlz Allowed." Like garlic, misogyny oozes out his pores, but the stinky man can't smell his foul odor. It's easy to blame our plight on bitches and hoes, and reassuring to believe that women who refuse our advances are lesbians or man-hating Feminazis. It takes an incredible amount of effort and energy to avoid the easy denunciations – the anger and frustration we experience has to go *somewhere* – but you must love and embrace womankind before they'll return the favor.

Mint-Condition Man

There are many advantages to dating a Mint-Condition Man. He is grateful and kind – if anything, too grateful and too kind. He doesn't talk dirty in the boudoir because his overwhelming urge is to shout, "I can't believe this is finally happening." A Mint-Condition Man is never sexually greedy, and will gladly reduce his *menage à trois* fantasies by thirty-three percent. Unfortunately, most women see his Mint-Condition status as disadvantageous: when you break in a new pair of dress shoes, you usually get a blister. Mint-Condition Man needs to be creatively truthful. If a woman inquires about his bedroom technique, he can truthfully reply, "No complaints thus far."

Ego Inflammation

Most single guys lack self-assuredness, but a rare few are unjustifiably confident in their abilities. Too much of a good thing is as useless as too little. Take Max (Jason Schwartzman), the star of *Rushmore*. Despite all odds, this tenth-grader pursues Ms. Cross, an elementary school teacher, and builds an aquarium to impress her. She eventually relents and kisses Max, but his wrong-headed and misdirected ego expenditure nearly costs him the more age-appropriate love of classmate Margaret.

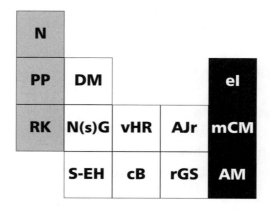

Figure 1: Periodic Table of Single Guys

SOME QUINTESSENTIAL SINGLE GUYS

Astute Brutes skulk in the dusty corners of pop culture, because most people prefer films featuring snooty cats and courageous dogs with celebrity voices, or films starring a shirtless Russell Crowe over *The Elephant Man*. There is a distinct lack of pizzazz to the phrase "the feel-okay movie of the year." Still, I've managed to locate a few fictional single guys to help clarify our world view.

Arno Strine, the protagonist of Nicholson Baker's novel *The Fermata,* is the most engaging – and morally confused – single guy in history. Arno has a special power – he can pause/stop time. He calls this state of affairs The Fold.

Arno uses The Fold to transcribe audiocassettes (his job) in half the normal time. He uses it to write his autobiography (the conceit of *The Fermata* is that it is a self-published novel about his experiences in The Fold). He uses it to calmly browse during the Christmas shopping rush, to let a bad mood at work pass, or analyze a revealing comment.

But mostly, he undresses women.

I have no urge to defend his actions (even Arno calls them indefensible), yet it's tough to dislike him. He fools the reader with constant introspection, his thoughtfulness somehow burying bad habits in white noise. It is the way in which Arno uses and abuses power (or doesn't, according to his convoluted, but consistent inner logic) that makes him an Astute Brute. He applies rules and ethics to a situation that lends itself to immorality: "In my place, some would toggle time and cheat on their Ph.D. orals or simply take money from open cash registers. Cheating and stealing don't tempt me though."

Arno doesn't have sex with any women in The Fold – he finds the thought appalling. But many of his Fold adventures are sick and depraved. He never embarrasses anyone, though – they never know what he's done. He, in his own bizarre way, is very respectful of the objects of his affection, if you can get past the initial violation.

Arno also explores what we might do in his situation. He asks various people what they would do in a hypothetical Fold. Sex and/or nudity-related ideas are always the first to emerge, followed closely by stealing.

Arno has confidence (beyond wanting to write an entire book about himself), but he speaks the language of the single guy. He's had but three long-term relationships (he's thirty-five). Curiously, he doesn't loathe solitude. "Loneliness makes you consider other people's lives, makes you more polite to those you deal with in passing, dampens irony and cynicism."

At the end of the novel, Arno accidentally transfers his powers to Joyce, a woman who, unlike his ex-girlfriend Rhody, doesn't see the "implied necrophilia" of fooling around in The Fold. Joyce's love is enough to ease the withdrawal pains of not being able to disrobe women any longer. I'm sure there's a lesson in there somewhere.

The best Astute Brutes aren't real, and Tintin is no exception. A creation of the late Belgium artist Hergé (a.k.a. Georges

Remi), Tintin is a blond, cowlicked journalist, a perpetual six-teen-year-old who goes all over the world on grand adven-tures. In strictly objective grade-school boy terms, he's the coolest ever.

Tintin is Astute (he uses cunning and costumes to trick adversaries) and Brute (he punches people and uses a gun when necessary) in perfect dosages. Still, Tintin has a funda-mental character flaw – he has never, ever had a love interest despite starring in twenty-two books. He has friends, like the alcoholic Captain Haddock, the absentminded Professor Calculus, and those meddling Thompson and Tompson twins. And of course, his trusty dog Snowy. But he doesn't kiss the girls and make them cry. There has never been so much as a floozy hinted at in the Tintin series, and let's face it, with a cute pooch and a great haircut, he wouldn't have had much trouble "picking up."

I'd prefer not to sully my childhood hero by pondering his sexual orientation, but clearly his ambiguity doesn't begin and end in the bedroom. In Paris, on February 3, 1998, the sixty-member Tintin Parliamentary Fan Club sponsored a debate about whether Tintin was right- or left-wing. This was done as part of the seventieth anniversary celebration for the little Belgium lad. The right argued that *Tintin in the Soviet Union* reveals his deep distaste for communism. Their opponents pointed out that in *Tintin and the Picaros*, he joins a leftist group of South American guerrillas and overthrows a military dictatorship. Clearly, Tintin has commitment issues.

As I think about it, I spent my formative years reading about a single guy getting into all sorts of wondrous adven-tures that were bereft of women. Perhaps I should have read *Archie* or *Love's Stories* instead.

One of the most popular television sitcoms of the nineties featured two incredible Astute Brutes. George Castanza (Jason Alexander) and Jerry of *Seinfeld* fame have probably done the most to further the philosophical development of the single guy. The pride George takes in being a loser ("Pity's very underrated. I like pity. It's good"), coupled with his self-awareness, makes him barely Brute, but at the extreme end of Astuteness. He has analyzed the logic of loserdom like few others, producing many memorable Castanza Koans in the process.

He put forth the "great meeting story theory" which posits that none of his relationships have worked out because the mechanism and manner in which he met the woman wasn't clever, bizarre, or dramatic. The snub (playing hard to get) doesn't work for him. He has dabbled in marine biology and Latvian Orthodoxy to impress women. He finds success only when he does the exact opposite of what his instincts suggest. There are Missing Posters at the post-office featuring a blurry photo of George's self-confidence. Upon learning that a boy French-kissed Elaine at his bar-mitzvah, George remarks incredulously, "Wow! I didn't try that 'til I was twenty-three." And he's never come to terms with his physical appearance. "I always get the feeling that when lesbians look at me, they're thinking, '*That's* why I'm not a heterosexual.'"

And yet, he has numerous relationships. He almost got married, for chrissakes!

Jerry and George are a team, and Jerry has also added to our understanding of the man-child. The episode where his brain and his penis play chess to decide if Jerry should keep dating a bimbo is the Astute Brute dichotomy rendered crudely but accurately (the brain wins). And his advice to George about the male gaze is classic: "Looking at cleavage is like looking at the sun! You don't stare at it! It's too risky! You get a sense of it, then you look away."

Proving single guys aren't the exclusive domain of North America is Adrian Mole. The creation of author Sue Townsend, Adrian is pseudo-Astute, a self-proclaimed intellectual who failed his "A" levels and whose only area of expertise is the Norwegian Leather Industry. After three decades, he still doesn't know that Eric Blair and George Orwell are the same person. He's not exactly Brutish, either. As he notes in *The Secret Diary of Adrian Mole Aged 13¾*, "I used to be the sort of boy who had sand kicked in his face, now I'm the sort of boy who watches somebody else have it kicked in their face."

Most Astute Brutes are good at self-reflection. Adrian is a rare breed; he can't see *any* of his nearly endless faults. He's arguably the worst poet in England, having once written an opus entitled *The Restless Tadpole*.

What makes him an honorary single guy is that he's pined after Pandora Braithwaite, his first true love, for nearly two decades. The apex (or nadir) of their carnal knowledge is a session of "extremely heavy petting" conducted at age fifteen. Like an insect trapped in amber, Adrian is immobilized by his infatuation.

In *Adrian Mole: The Cappuccino Years*, my sympathy for thirty-year-old Adrian finally wanes. He divorces a beautiful, smart, and wealthy Nigerian named Jo-Jo (who is four inches taller than Adrian) due to irreconcilable differences – Adrian dislikes the way she sneezes.

Adrian is balding. He is on Prozac. He's cheap and selfish. He has British teeth. He should be happy to meet any female with opposable thumbs, yet makes a detailed list of reasons not to date a nurse named Lucy. (Number five: "Prefers normal to lemon Jif.")

Despite Pandora's sham marriage and her long-term affair with an older professor, Adrian's passion remains unwavering. "I *know* that I am her only true love, and that she is mine. We are Arthur and Guinevere, Romeo and Juliet, Charles and Camilla."

LANGUAGE OF LOVE SPOKEN MOST EXCELLENTLY HERE: COMMUNICATION

Most single guys are functionally illiterate when it comes to body language. We understand public displays of rejection, but fail to understand that the semaphore of the sweaty brow, a lake of underarm perspiration, or nervous head twitching might be unappealing to the opposite sex. Here's why: evolutionary biology postulates that beneficial traits (running fast, opening pickle jars, crushing beer tins on forehead) will be favored over bad traits (running slowly, dying young, leaving the toilet seat up). This is called genetic fitness. From an evolutionary standpoint, a prehistoric man displaying too much fear around women created the impression he'd have even more trouble battling a woolly mammoth. His genes faded.

But not all of this female-related foreboding is our fault. The autonomic nervous system provides us with a "fight-or-flight" option at no extra charge. Single guys have a predisposition towards the "flight" option. If that weren't bad enough, not only are we trying to overcome a reflex designed to save our lives, we're also battling Lennie Syndrome: "Gosh, she was purty. I jus' wanted to feel that girl's dress – jus' wanted to pet it like a mouse. Now's she's gone. I done a bad thing."

Besides, women can smell fear.

Single guys are a little better with conversation. They're smart enough not to use pickup lines such as:

> » Hi! The voices in my head told me to come talk to you.
> » Was it love at first sight, or should I walk by again?
> » Pardon me, I've lost my phone number, could I borrow yours?
> » Let's play post office. You lick me and I'll deliver.
> » Great Manolo Blahniks!
> » I'm Fred Flintstone and I'd like to make your Bedrock.
> » Would you like to see my etchings?
> » Excuse me, do you live around here often?
> » If I follow you home, will you keep me?
> » The word of the day is "legs." Let's go spread the word.
> » That outfit must make a lot of noise in the dryer.
> » You know what I like about you? My arms.
> » My name is Ryan, but you can call me tonight.
> » Hi. You'll do.
> » Please?

Avoiding stupid sentences is good, but the strong, silent method has limitations. For those whose grasp on the language of love is pidgin at best, I am proud to debut romantic Esperanto. It's like Magnetic Poetry or those monkeys with all the typewriters. Use these words and phrases, and eventually you'll say something profound:

Me Talk to Pretty Girl One Day

Basic Greetings & Civilities
Hello.
How are you?
I'm fine.
Excuse me.
Thank you.

ADVANCED:
· I promise to pay the dry-cleaning bill.

Small Talk
What is your name?
My name is…Slim Shady.
Do you have?…
No?
No?!
No?!?
Are you sure?

ADVANCED:
Are you very sure?
I did not realize the angry bouncer is your boyfriend.

Language Difficulties
I understand.
I don't understand.
You're lesbian *and* celibate?

Accommodation
Bed and breakfast.
Breakfast in bed.
Do you have a room?
I have many extra clean towels.
And a spare toothbrush.

ADVANCED:
My abode or yours?
My hovercraft is full of eels. No wait, I mean…
I am no longer infected.

Getting Around
I would like to go…
Where is the:
» airport
» station
» taxi stand
» subway
» Secret Land of Og
» railway station
» department store window full of nude
mannequins
What time will the train leave, Mr. Conductor?

ADVANCED:
Will there be attractive single women on the train?
For seat next to her, how much bribe?

Around Town
    What time does [insert place] open? Close?
        Bank.
        Beach.
        Museum.
        Blanket.
        Market.
        Bingo.

Shopping
    How much?
    Too expensive.

ADVANCED:
    I'd love to shop for shoes all day.

Health & Emergencies
    I need a doctor.
    What is up, doctor?
    Trust me, I'm a doctor. Please disrobe.

ADVANCED:
    Where is the all-night pharmacy?
    A week's delay is hardly worth worrying about.
    Are you sure the indicator turned green?

Time
   What's the time?
   Today.
   Tomorrow.
   Yesterday.

ADVANCED:
   I do not comprehend, "When hell freezes over."
   I do not comprehend, "Over my dead body."

Days of the Week
   Are you free on Sunday?
   How about Monday?
   Perhaps Tuesday?
   Might I inquire as to your Wednesday availability?
   M'lady, I beseech you to meet with me this Thursday.
   What, pray tell, do your Friday plans consist of?
   Could you delay your intensive shampoo regime and
   partake in the legitimate theatre this Saturday?

ADVANCED:
   How does dinner and a movie on the evening of
   March 12, 2058 sound?

My final communication suggestion involves the written word. Single guys are constantly battling their excitement. Forget the three-day moratorium on calling a woman back; waiting two rings before answering the phone is difficult enough. Patience is at a premium and some men express their feelings too soon for even the most Harlequin-saturated female to appreciate. Using the word "love" too early, even if you mean it, can be real trouble. I realize I railed against eu-phemisms in **Past, Present, and Accounted For**, but throwing around the "L" word is often interpreted by women as a sign that the man is some sort of emotional leech. While true, it is important to pretend otherwise. Wait until the relationship is so entrenched that finding someone else poses too much has-sle for her.

Until the right moment, consider instead love's timid un-derstudy "luv" – perfect for writing Luv Letters and signing birthday cards. By altering one vowel and removing another, you effectively defuse the power of that four-letter word. Here's a quick list demonstrating the efficacy of "luv":

> Incorrect: Yesterday, during dinner, when you passed me the pepper shaker without being prompted, I realized that I love you.
> Correct: I luv the way you spice up my day!
>
> Incorrect: Last night, when we finally transferred our spiritual platitudes onto a physical plane, I re-alized that the magical aura surrounding us is neither mere yearning or base desire, but the warm red frenchfry lamp glow of deepest transcendent love.
> Correct: Luv the boom-boom, toots.
>
> Incorrect: Donating one of your kidneys to my mother brought tears to my eyes – tears that reflect my deep gratitude and love – yes, LOVE – for you.
> Correct: Thanx for tossing up one of your pee-pee or-gans to my ma. Luv, Ryan.

SINGLE-MINDED: EMOTIONAL RESCUE

It's time for a quick tour through the mind of an Astute Brute. To paraphrase Hunter S. Thompson, "We were somewhere around Barstow on the edge of the desert when the depression began to take hold."

Yes, we're all sad, but it varies from guy to guy. It's a bit like tartan patterns – the weeping and moaning appears similar, but there are subtle differences between, say, a whimper, and a sob.

Depression is a very common affliction, ranging from the mildest forms (ex-girlfriend's revenge) to severe cases where medication is required. However, there is nothing funny about Prozac or therapy, unless Frasier Crane or Bob Hartley is involved. I have always been in favor of toughing things out, but the Nietzsche approach (Whatever does not kill me makes me stronger) doesn't work for everyone. And some women favor pre-shrunk men.

Prevention is the best way of battling the blahs. Most Astute Brutes manage to avoid serious mental illness through early identification. With a few precautions and a firm grasp of the warning signs, single guys can look forward to slowly losing their will to live in a relaxed and painless fashion.

There are also syndromes and diseases unique to those "between relationships." One of the most common afflictions is Rain Man syndrome. This occurs when single men chant nonsense: "Definitely single for 327 days. Definitely depressing. Definitely time to stop counting toothpicks and find a girlfriend." It is annoying but harmless.

Some men appear to have mononucleosis. But mono is a kissing disease. These guys sleep in so as to leave less daytime to deal with.

Next is the Guillotine Swish: the chilling moment in a conversation (with someone of the fairer sex) when a man realizes that in a split-second Ms. Robspierre will mention her boyfriend, and he is powerless to stop her.

> Him: Nice weather today, isn't it?
> Her: Yes, it's almost as nice as when I went to California with (*swish*) my boyfriend.

Another disease is Ringcheck. This mental tic has less to do with how long a guy has been single and more to do with his age. Ringcheck is an obsessive-compulsive disorder, triggered by diamonds and the occasional cubic zirconia. The concentration of Ringcheck-provoking molecules in the bloodstream builds over time, lurking benignly until age twenty. Guys wave goodbye to their teen years and suddenly start to notice women their own age with wedding rings. Seeing a woman – who wouldn't date them to begin with – rendered completely unattainable causes a kind of anaphylactic shock. Often the victim will break out in hives, his throat swelling and his eyes watering.

The more intense the disbelief, the more likely the ring will disappear, believes the Ringcheck sufferer. Wedding bands cause irritation, since these small bits of gold and diamond represent severe fantasy extinction. A typical single guy can't attract an unattached women, so why would a woman leave her betrothed for him? Still, a few brave, tortured souls (like myself) continue to carry the torch for claimed women. Instead of acting on these urges, I have sublimated them through bad fiction. In my latest "romance" novel (*Behind the Automatic Garage Door*), the main character,

Ryan Smith, overturns the bourgeois morality held so dear by most engaged young ladies. In this excerpt, Matilda is rapidly repressing her upcoming wedding:

> "Oh Ryan!" Matilda cried passionately, tossing her engagement ring into the corner with the same reckless abandon she had used to toss her clothes there only moments earlier. Her bosom heaved as she stepped closer and began to....

Men who have been single for more than three months become anxious over condom expiry dates. Those single for more than twelve months are susceptible to Hysterical Relationship Syndrome (HRS). While not yet recognized by the *Diagnostical Statistical Manual IV: Return of the Asylum Avengers,* I assure you this disease is quite real. In a hysterical pregnancy, a woman will gain weight and mimic all the symptoms of having a bun in the oven. HRS is similar, the only difference being that a hysterical pregnancy can occur *despite* an absence of intercourse, while HRS develops *because* of an absence of intercourse.

While I have not yet had a hysterical girlfriend (not to be confused with a girlfriend who's hysterical), a friend of mine I'll call "Ryan" occasionally suffers from phantom female delusions. Like Big Bird's Snuffleupagus, Ryan's "girlfriend" is vividly described, but never seen. In order to convince his friends that he's not some kind of weirdo loser, he often says things such as:

> » "I just got off the phone with her."
> » "She just left."
> » "Here's the toothbrush she uses when she stays over."

The most insidious disease is *Single-itis* (Si1). Like malaria, it slowly saps the strength of the host and alters brain chemistry. Eventually, sufferers lose the energy and inspiration to escape the magnetic field of single life, no matter how many issues of *Happy Couples Buying Things Together* they might read.

Si1 is the disease that causes an otherwise functional, normal male to memorize every Monty Python routine, learn to speak Klingon, or devote his life to playing Ultima Online. Single men retreat into specialties because it feels good to be the master of something. My cultural outlet of choice is *The Simpsons*. Take my advice, you don't want me to prove my expertise. For reasons forever lost to me, women don't care if Homer once consumed a ten-pound bag of flour when no other food was available. Thankfully, in 1998, I kicked the habit.

Not every D&D nerd is unsuccessful with the ladies. From January until August of 2000, I lived with three guys who played Magic: The Gathering. Magic is a card-based fantasy game where you cast spells and summon creatures to drain your opponent's "life force." They played it constantly, and discussed it with an equal fervor. Yet, these guys were all socially adjusted and capable of sustained, meaningful conversations. And yes, they all had girlfriends.

Successfully integrating witches and warlocks is rare, however. Undetected Si1 can cause untold problems. Frequent self-examinations are recommended. To reduce the occurrences of Si1, I have created a pamphlet detailing the horrors of this shocking disease.

Do you suffer from Single-itis? Maybe you think that Single-itis only happens to "other people." Well here, in their own words, are unrehearsed testimonials from sufferers of this dreaded affliction.

I never thought it could happen to me. I had a great job and an active social life. I attended church almost every Sunday. Then one day I looked in the mirror and realized I WAS ALL ALONE. I guess in the excitement of career and hobbies, I'd neglected to find myself a girlfriend.
— Bob, age 25

Some people refuse to admit they're single. They create elaborate lies and excuses to cover up "their little secret."

I'd tell my friends that I was "busy" every so often, in order to create the impression that I had a girlfriend. But in reality, I'd stay at home, eat corn chips, and watch re-runs of Manimal. *I was trapped in a shame spiral that I couldn't escape. If only someone had reached out to me. If only....*
— David, age 23¾

Others react with anger, lashing out at the people they used to care for.

Sometimes I miss my ex-girlfriend, but my aim is improving.
— Name and age withheld upon request

Others react with self-deprecating humor.

People often ask me what I'm like in bed. Last week I finally admitted, "I sleep on my left side and I occasionally snore."
— Brad, age 28

Evidence for Si1 has been accumulating for over a decade, yet it went unrecognized by the *New England Journal of Medicine* until April of 2000. Had Si1 been identified sooner, thousands might have been saved through early detection programs. Controversy over Si1 continues, but for those who suffer from it, the frustration is real.

I was desperate to find a girlfriend. I'd pretend to be interested in anything that might win me favor with females. The list was endless: ballet, films with plots, walks on the beach, foreplay....
— Grant, age unknown

Luckily, things are changing. There is now help and hope available for long-suffering single men. Being girlfriend-challenged is no longer your fault. Don't try to carry the burden of shame and the weight of the world on your mortal shoulders. Being shy is now a legitimate medical excuse for not having a girlfriend.

Fighting Single-itis is difficult. But it can be successfully treated without drugs like rohypnol. Free clinics have been set up in most major cities to help detect and reverse its effects. If you exhibit any or all of the danger signs, or know someone who does, help them shake this debilitating disease forever by seeking help.

When I first came to the Si1 Quarantine Facility, I was pretty belligerent. I mean, imagine how you would feel if you were told by a complete stranger that you had a serious "problem." But now I realize that I was living in denial. The trained professionals at the Facility gave me the help I needed to get back on my feet again. Now I practically have a harem. Thank you.
— Richard, age 29

Donations for the Si1 Institute of Research are always appreciated. Please give generously so that we may continue investigating this tragic and confusing disease.

THE ELEVEN DANGER SIGNS OF SINGLE-ITIS

- Feelings of sadness or irritation
- Changes in weight or appetite
- Female deficiency syndrome
- Loss of interest or pleasure in activities once enjoyed
- Changes in sleeping patterns
- Feeling guilty, hopeless, or worthless
- Strongly identifying with Nick Drake, Ian Curtis, or Lou Barlow
- Inability to concentrate, remember things, or make decisions
- A general and lasting feeling of hopelessness
- Misdirected anger
- Propensity toward humor-book writing

MARRIAGE HAS TEETH AND HIM BITE HOT

Marriage has always occupied a unique position on the ideological mantle of long-suffering single guys. While it purports to offer total salvation from loneliness, it taketh away many other freedoms. (I see marriage as too much of a gamble for a pessimist like myself. I know how much trouble I have maintaining a long-term relationship. This matrimony thing presents a double-or-nothing proposition of pain and suffering. If it works, great, if it fails . . . well, I'd rather not think about it.)

Single guys created a mental retreat called the Very Lonely Planet. Wedded folk build very real, geographical enclaves. They reside within a grotesque arrangement of houses and oversized retail outlets called "the suburbs." They navigate this territory in boxy land-rovers called "SUVs" or "minivans." These vehicles are also used to transport tiny, screaming pink aliens. Married couples even have their own language, saying things like "We loved Bermuda" and "We had pasta for lunch."

Because of zoning laws and linguistic impediments, meaningful communication between the haves and the have-nots soon becomes impossible. I realize there are some advantages to substituting single life for Sex Land (your mileage may vary), but abandoning the single buddies who got you through tough times is very rude.

After spending so long trying to find the perfect match and failing, you'll excuse me if I'm a bit skeptical toward those who claim otherwise. Obviously they've been invaded by body snatchers. And I don't mean to scare you needlessly, but when you become married, staying home and watching television becomes a *very exciting activity indeed.*

Despite the low success rate – experts now predict that within twenty years, 112 percent of all marriages will end in divorce – the ball and chain keeps clanking. Now, don't get me wrong, some of my best friends are married. No longer the domain of Christians and pigeons, lifelong monogamy is claiming certifiable hipsters, scenesters, and Munsters. The best minds of my generation are being destroyed by matrimony, and I'm howling mad.

I have trouble integrating the constraints and traditions of marriage with the perceived modernism of my friends. I think part of the problem is semantics. There is little tangible difference between "long-term girlfriend" and "wife" (well, until the lawyers get involved), but the psychological rifts are enormous. I like the idea that common-law marriages just sort of happen, much like milk expiring or a library book becoming due. There is little fanfare or ceremony, which appeals to me greatly. To me, the storybook wedding is the exclusive reserve of science fiction.

My other fears about marriage stem from the fact that every other grown-up privilege I've been granted has disappointed. I often consider reneging on my dues to Club Adult. While the recruitment pamphlet convinced me that membership had its privileges (the right to vote, the ability to buy alcohol legally, the whole age-of-consent thing), I didn't bother to read the fine print (paying taxes, cleaning up after oneself, and being forced to say, "that's what the kids are doing" with alarming frequency).

Still, Club Adult has managed to impart some wisdom (and a fifteen percent discount at participating Ikea locations).

Since there is a chance my future wife might be reading this very paragraph (Hi there! You've made an excellent decision. I like long walks on the beach and candlelit dinners), I would like to provide my official stance on marriage.

The precedent for this opinion was set by a May 17, 1997 ruling, wherein I, Ryan S. Bigge, did in fact attend a proper wedding, and wherein the ceremony contained sixty-five people and the reception contained eighty-five people. The defendant will admit the event itself was fairly exciting, even for a bitter old man like him. Let it be known he had to wear a tuxedo, but despite the penguin suit and his inherent cynicism, he had an okay time, enhanced tremendously by an open bar. Despite plenty of free booze, I managed to catalogue the myriad limitations of a traditional wedding. Simply put, I dislike the muss and fuss required:

» engagement announcement in newspaper
» picking a minister
» picking a fight with the minister
» watching reruns of *Yes, Prime Minister*
» mailing invitations
» bridal shower
» cold shower
» selecting a wedding dress
» choosing an MC who will thoroughly embarrass you
» choosing a wedding mascot
» choosing salt (iodized or not)
» deciding whether or not to put rice in the salt shakers
» deciding what type of rice to put in said salt shakers (basmati, brown, converted, or instant)
» finding a few good men, a pretty good man, and a best man

» providing at least one of the following distractions:
  • in-laws fighting over where to sit
  • in-laws fighting over whose granddaughter is cuter
  • in-laws fighting over tiny scraps of colored paper
  • a crazy drunken uncle (lampshade optional but it must not clash with the tuxedo, the wedding dress, or the china pattern)
» rehearsing the wedding
» synchronizing the lasers
» finding a way to toss the garter without requiring an entertainment license
» deciding how many bitter divorcées should be in attendance
» hiring a referee for the bouquet toss
» ignoring the groom's request to put a green plastic army man on top of the cake

A death-row prisoner chooses his method of execution, specifies his marriage preference. I would tolerate eloping to Vegas, wherein a Vegas wedding definition involves some or all of the following items:

» plane tickets
» fifteen minutes to spare
» toothbrush (optional)

Perhaps I'm asking too much. By making some concessions to marriage, I am implicitly suggesting that a woman would be willing to live with me all day, every day, until one of us dies – hopefully of natural causes. Add the Vegas stipulation and it gets even more impossible.

Most women want their wedding to be an unforgettably special day. Cajoled by *Expensive Marriage Magazine*, women (and some men) start believing that they actually want a fancy ceremony, the sort where food is served on Royal Chinet paper plates and the groom wears clean and/or properly ironed pants. My response to such a suggestion is: "That's what second marriages are for." By the time you get around to *Marriage II: Wrath of Khan*, the man will have enough money, maturity, and patience to consider a conventional wedding.

Sadly, even non-traditional women balk at Vegas. I will grant you that it's not the most romantic of places, and that the serum count of schmaltz is high, but to me cheesy is all right – arguing with the caterer over edam hors d'oeuvres is not.

Marriage is ridiculous. So is Vegas. Oh look! There's peanut butter in my chocolate! Where else can you get conjoined and then place money at 2:1 odds (offer invalid to those from the 90210 zip code) on whether or not your marriage will last? In what other city will you be given an opportunity to try and win back the money you've spent on achieving matrimonial bliss? Where else will the ceremony take less time than the good parts of the honeymoon? (Respected physicians with ice-cold stethoscopes recommend foreplay.)

Vegas might be as spiritually satisfying as a disposable lighter, but secular rituals do have certain advantages. If there is a god, why does he or she allow us to suffer thusly? It's time for a ceremonial vow that begins, "We are gathered here today, in the sight of Robert Goulet and inexpensive shrimp cocktails, to unite Ryan and the woman currently standing beside Ryan in unholy matrimony...."

DIVINE INTERVENTION

There are few relevant institutions in the life of the single guy. Government has little meaning in a society that operates on the "every man for himself" principle. Single guys have failed to form a special interest group to lobby for the mandatory, year 'round placement of mistletoe. We lack a keen grasp of the body politic. Even if we managed to elect a president that understood our pain, his position would likely be titular (giggle).

Spirituality, however, remains somewhat important to single guys. Since 1998, I've been celibate for religious reasons.

God hates me.

Many single guys identify with aspects of Christianity, usually in the personage of Jesus, who reportedly died without having sex. Behaving like a self-righteous martyr is appealing and we're willing to follow anyone who will lead us to the promised land.

But not every single guy is interested in sacraments, confession booths, or Catholic school girls. There is a growing resurgence in the popularity of Buddhism, based partly on the successful conversion of Adam Yauch (*I'm Beastie Boy/number three/My new religion/is interplanetary*). The Buddha's belief that "all life is suffering" has a certain resonance.

A few single guys use the stars and celestial bodies (giggle) as oracles. But most Astute Brutes are scared of anything vaguely New Agey. The problem with horoscopes (beyond being complete rubbish) is their lack of precision. Astute Brutes are not that interested in spending a lot of time sifting through tea leaves. We want clear and direct advice:

> » Taurus (April 20-May 20): You will go to Spain to fight matadors.
> » Pisces (Feb 19-March 20): You like fish. Even anchovies.
> » Cancer (June 21-July 22): You are thinking of a number between one and ten. It is eight.

Instead, we get gobbledygook:

> » Capricorn (Feb 19-March 20) Conjunct ascendant chakra. Purple monkey dishwasher.

Confirmed cynics tend to reserve their faith for only one particular astrological bearer of news – Haley's comet. Single guys watch the progress of Haley's comet with great interest, since we strongly identify with a phenomenon that only comes once every seventy-three years.

Despite Schwa (who provide Alien Defense Kits) and the Church of the SubGenius ("An Order of Scoffers and Blasphemers, dedicated to Total Slack"), there appears to be no religion perfectly suited for us.

Until now.

Our prayers were answered, when, after a month-long expedition led by Tia "Relic Hunter" Carrere, a *Single Guy Bible* was discovered in a cave near Piltdown, England. The existence of such a tome should come as little surprise, given all those other versions, including:

> » the King James Version
> » the Hoboken Version
> » Mattel's Speak and Spell Bible (the Lord says, "No," the follower says, "Yes," the sinner says, "Sorry")
> » Bible 2.01

Unfortunately, much of the papyrus text is partially or completely obscured by tear stains, but I am pleased to present the surviving remnants.

Lonely Old Testament

Genesis (Post Peter Gabriel)
First Book of Moses, Chapter One
In the beginning there was a single guy in a garden, or a gazebo or something. And God said let there be light, and great whales, and breakfast cereals, and llamas and so on. Adam soon realized that all the animals were in pairs and he wasn't. He became lonely, so God yanked out one of Adam's ribs and created Eve. (Some claim Lilith was the first woman, but she had some problems dealing with authority, and was last seen driving a blue, 1966 T-Bird Convertible toward an escarpment.)

And Adam sayeth, "Hey good work, God, she's naked."

And God replied, "Whoops, I guess I made a mistake. Wait a minute. I never make mistakes. That'd be blasphemous. I'm perfect. And omniscient, a word I just learned from *Reader's Digest*'s "Improve Your Word Power." And He quickly covered his tracks and invented the first Wonderbra (you'll wonder what's underneath it). Then God created the first dating game. *All right, Eve, will you choose Bachelor #1, Bachelor #1, or Bachelor #1?* Eve, however, was underwhelmed by Adam's fig leaf and chose none of the above, deciding instead to have a fling with a snake.

Adam pleaded with God, saying, "Come on, try again. Please. I've got fifteen more ribs. I'm a desperate man."

God shrugged and walked away, deep in thought, wondering if He could make a rock so big that even He couldn't lift it.

Undeterred, Adam held his breath until he turned blue. God relented and fixed Adam up on a dinner date. However, Adam was a klutz and accidentally spilled red wine all over Eve's new frock. Last supper indeed.

Chapter Six
And then it started to rain. With extreme prejudice.. So God pulled Moses aside and pitched him this idea He'd been saving for a special occasion: The Ark. "Listen, how about you and the missus and a few close members of the animal kingdom go on a three-hour cruise?"

Forty days and a divorce later, Moses was permitted to kiss sweet terra firma again. Moments later, someone made a lame sheep joke.

New Testament (not the metal band)

The Revelations of St John the Divine
Not all men think The Three Stooges are funny.

Erizarisus, Chapter 25, verse 94
And thou shall not massage the feet of Uma Thurman, for if her husband catches you he will exercise great vengeance upon you with furious rebukes. Or throw your ass over a balcony.

Proverbs 7
David the Piously Single decided to drown his sorrows with elderberry wine at the 700 nightclub. A few hours later, behold, despite all odds, a woman comes to meet him, dressed as a harlot and cunning of heart. So she seizes him and kisses him, and with a brazen face she says to him: "Come, let us drink our fill of love until morning. Let us delight ourselves with caresses." Unfortunately, the booze proved to be a pox upon David, and though the spirit was willing, the flesh was weak.

Book of Jason, The Final Chapter
By this point everyone was getting tired of commandments and plagues and the wailing and the gnashing of teeth. All this faith and devotion and not one sign from the heavens.

Everyone was about to go home and convert to Zoroastrianism when suddenly they saw Him standing above them. The line of the ocean cut the sky. The ocean swelled as the gates of the holy city descended. He passed the pinnacles of the temple of the money lenders. He rose about the spires of a church and spoke.
"Remember, I am coming soon! I bring with me the reward that will be given to each man as his conduct deserves. I am the Alpha and the Omega, the First and the Last, the Beginning and the End! The grace of Howard Roark be with you all. Amen!"

Then there was only the ocean and the sky and the figure of Howard Roark.

Epilogue
Those who recognized the reference to Ayn Rand's *The Fountainhead* were pleasantly surprised to discover that God had a sense of humor. They laughed heartily, their faith renewed everlasting and eternal. The remaining philistines – numbering in the millions – slowly nodded their heads in mock comprehension before deferring to blind faith. They hoped all would be revealed in the afterlife. It wasn't.

I believe this bible is fundamental to Astute Brute history and philosophy. We must uncover the lessons contained within. In an effort to help you retain and better understand this new religion, I've created some Single Guy Bible Study Questions:

Improve Your Word Power

1) What is fornication?
   A) sexual relations between unmarried people
   B) a starlike object that is the source of intense electromagnetic radiation

2) What is atonement?
   A) any electronic device having only two terminals that allows current to flow in only one direction
   B) to make amends

3) What is Lent?
   A) a British nobleman ranking between marquis and viscount
   B) the period from Ash Wednesday to Easter, of which the forty weekdays are observed as a time of fasting and penitence

4) Who is Nebuchadnezzar?
   A) King of the Assyrians
   B) a triple-decker sandwich

Things to Think About

1) Should God have smitten Commander Zoltan with the immutable rod of Denglatron? Why or why not?
2) Find one example of foreshadowing.
3) Is Mom and Dad's divorce *really* my fault?

Daily Reflections

1) Prayer might help.
2) Nearly half of the Commandments remain relevant in today's hurly-burly world. Can you guess which ones?
3) "Hey God, what's the deal with all the suffering? I mean, come on." Discuss.

Further Ahead

1) Your local library has many books about religion.
2) Do you believe in God? Why or why not? Use the other side of the page if you require more space.
3) Make a diorama about Jesus. Be sure to ask your mom or dad's permission before using scissors, glue, or thumb tacks.
4) Have you ever seen God? If not, hold this page close to your nose, slowly move it away and suddenly, God will appear!
5) Was the Ayn Rand reference in the Bible excerpt reasonable or is the author trying to cop some Dennis Miller-style 'tude?
6) Who is John Galt?

Too Far Ahead

1) Why or why not?
2) True or false?
3) Explain in more detail.

SAD BASTARDS OF YOUNG: MUSIC

Garbologists sift through coffee grounds and eggshells. Volcanologists scrutinize tectonic plates and liquid hot magma. Singleologists riffle through CD collections.

Glossy magazines (*Stuff*) and self-help books (*Mars, Venus, the Cook, the Thief, His Wife, and Her Lover*) have failed us, and there is no male equivalent to the chick flick (although *Titanic* taught us that if you only have sex once before you die, be sure it's with Kate Winslet). Music, by default, is the font of masculine confession and redemption; flagellation and salvation. We spend hours studying these hymns, interpreting their vagaries as if they were scripture. (Thus, when a woman says, "I like all kinds of music" it is as nonsensical and as blasphemous as proclaiming, "I like all kinds of religion.")

Singleologists spend their time cataloguing a genre I've dubbed Sad Bastard. This type of music can take many forms – jazz, country, new country, hip-hop, goth, classical, reggae, electronica, meringue – but the message is basically the same: why oh why oh why oh why me?

Every generation sends a hero up the pop charts; in the early 1990s, Astute Brutes sent a bespectacled anti-hero up the Sad Bastard chart: Lou Barlow. Lou-ness was inevitable. Lonely, university-educated, middle-class men yearned for songs created by sad, university-educated, middle-class musicians. The name of this Astute Brute-specific flavor of Sad Bastard was indie-rock. It used thin, trebly jolts of melody and feedback to convey its message of decreased expectations.

Indie-rock simmered during the 1980s, as bands like

Galaxie 500, the Meat Puppets, the Minutemen, the Replacements, Hüsker Dü, and Sonic Youth schlepped across America in decrepit vans, proselytizing. One such band, Dinosaur Jr., featured our anti-hero Lou on bass. Lou and guitarist J. Mascus didn't always get along. Mascus removed Lou from the band in 1989.

This made Lou sad.

Lou began recording and singing under a number of different names, including Sentridoh, the Folk Implosion, Deluxx Folk Implosion, and Lou Barlow and Friends. His main band was Sebadoh, with whom he sang about being kicked out of Dinosaur Jr. ("The Freed Pig") and about his girlfriend Kathleen leaving him for another guy ("Soul and Fire" and "Brave New Love" and "Willing to Wait" and "Two Years, Two Days" and "Rebound"). Barlow is the Stephen King of indie-rock – there are at least six Sebadoh albums, three Folk Implosion albums, and one album each from Sentridoh and Lou Barlow and Friends.

Lou was able to crank out so much material because of his love of lo-fi. Short for low-fidelity, lo-fi guys (and gals) championed the use of inexpensive recording equipment such as four-track recorders. Lo-fi created a group of musicians and fans with a fetish for the crackle and hiss of a 78 phonograph. It might be difficult to believe, but murkiness or tape hiss can augment the emotional intent of some songs. Like the clicks, pops, and static of old blues records, sound degradation became part of the listening experience.

Also known as "home recordings," lo-fi allowed a more intimate connection with the listener. It was easy to picture this music being recorded at three a.m., in the singer's bedroom or basement. Lo-fi was the audio equivalent of a zine – a diary excerpt set to music, with all the positives and negatives this implied. Rock lyrics are often vague and open to interpretation ("You're my wonderwall"), while lo-fi was starkly honest and uncomortably personal – dates, locations, and ex-girlfriends were named. Lo-fi could be self-indulgent – songs about rainy days and smoking pot – but the spontaneity and charm contrasted nicely the sterile, too-perfect studio albums. (Even superstar Beck recorded a lo-fi album entitled *One Foot in the Grave*, featuring the anti-hit, "Asshole.")

Not all love songs have to emulate Wham!'s "Careless Whisper." Lo-fi practitioner Will Oldham possesses a voice that cracks, twists, and strains on high notes, but he sings anyway, allowing himself the luxury of vulnerability. And you have to have a certain catch in your voice to warble, "When you have no one/no one can hurt you." Adding to the joylessness, his music label is called Drag City – home of other unhappy artists like Smog and Flying Saucer Attack. Despite the downbeat message, lo-fi *could* cheer you up – it proved someone else had it worse than you (i.e., manic-depressive musician Daniel Johnston).

This should surprise no one, but indie-rock was as self-reflexive as the guys who composed it. In the song "Plumb Line," the Archers of Loaf sang "she's an indie-rocker/and nothing's gonna stop her." King Lou penned the Sebadoh song "Gimmie Indie Rock" which served as a self-aggrandizing history: "It's the new generation/of electric white boy blues." To paraphrase the Bloodhound Gang, indie-rock was not black like Barry White, but white like Frank Black. At least we admitted it. (Indie-rock was also a male fiefdom, which is not discussed quite as often.)

The indie-rock community did a few good things. It redefined sex appeal, as mousy women with black-framed cat eye glasses and thrift store t-shirts became the bee's knees. Lo-fi championed the Do-It-Yourself ethos of punk. And there was a certain lack of pretension in the scene, although Indier-than-Thou priests quickly excommunicated any band that "sold out" or otherwise found favor with the hoi polloi.

Further proving his introspective nature, Sir Lou, under the Sentridoh umbrella, released "Losercore," a lo-fi anthem that damned the movement with faint praise ("Give this loser half control"). Indie-rock, especially lo-fi, is Astute glucose: thought rock. Indie superstars Pavement used big words (docent, chalice, quasar, terrarium, dashikis, jitney) and obtuse phrases (fruit-covered nails; Zurich is stained; serpentine pad; incandescent guillotine; epileptic surgeons). The level of Brute in the music varied, from the lukewarm (Lou Barlow constantly apologizing during his concerts) to red hot (the ironic swagger of blues boy Jon Spencer). For the most part, indie-rock cultivated an anti-rock star posture, as it gave the finger to stadium-filling rock bands who danced upon our paycheck. Our heroes wore t-shirts and jeans – nary a sequin in sight. They made low-key music videos, and sometimes they didn't even play their "hit" song(s) at their live shows.

The divide between performer and fan was slight, and both indie-rock and its scratchy cousin lo-fi encouraged its fans (either directly or indirectly) to become part of the problem. Since anyone with a few hundred dollars and a rudimentary knowledge of guitar theory could make an album, there were many anyones that did.

And so, with heaps of support from my friend/bass player/drummer Graeme Scott, The Plantains formed in 1996. Drawing heavily from the Pixies, *Bee Thousand*-era Guided by

Voices, and the Jesus and Mary Chain, we were a lean, mean, indie-rock machine that hit you square in the chest and threw you backwards.

I'm supposed to say I started a band because I had something vital and important to express through music. Which was true, I suppose, although our quasi-quasi-quasi-hit song "Hush Puppy Love" didn't exactly ponder the metaphysical certitude of Wittgenstein's *Tractatus Logico-Philosophicus*:

(to be sung in a droll deadpan, with the sort of ironic sneer that was so popular back in the mid-90s)

Verse

> *Fuzzy dice on the dashboard*
> *fuzz guitar and three chords*
> *running lights on your Hyundai*
> *Don'tcha know I'm a fun-guy*

Pre-chorus

> *Hey baby*
> *I got something to say*
> *I love you maybe*
> *hey baby*

Chorus

> *It was a suburban romance*
> *love in corduroy pants*
> *It was a suburban romance*
> *love in corduroy pants*

Verse

> *Watching soaps on a forty-inch Hitachi*
> *I love your hibachi*
> *you're my bar-bee-cutie*
> *always smiling and never moody*

repeat pre-chorus and chorus

Verse

> *Beanbag chairs and velvet art*
> *sipping lemonade and playing lawn darts*
> *all my friends just give me flack*
> *'cause I'm trapped in your cul-de-sac*

repeat pre-chorus and chorus

chorus addendum

> *I hope our love will last*
> *'cause I dearly love the middle class*

Being more honest, the band (which featured shiny guitars, snappy threads, and brightly colored plumage) was inspired by those screaming women watching the Beatles on Ed Sullivan. The Plantains was one of my first attempts to boost my Brute ranking. Toward this end, I purchased a pair of shiny blue pleather pants. It wasn't wasted money either, as the pants helped broker an actual date. Allow me the indulgence of repeating that thought: *the shiny pants helped broker an actual date.*

This would turn out to be an isolated incident, however. With indie-rock, one of the most enduring urban myths of the twentieth century – the groupie – often failed to materialize.

Rock journalists and commoners alike testify time and again that the high frequencies emitted by rock bands seem to:

» make the elastic of panties disintegrate
» cause the entire apparatus to become airborne
  (à la Tom Jones, et al.)
» cause pre-emptive underwear amnesia

None of the above came true. We did not get to meet Cynthia Plaster Caster, and had to be content with an incident involving some Silly Putty.

On the plus side, if something bad happened, at least you got a song out of it. In August of 1998, having depleted the list of constructive things to do with my life, I fell for a cashier at the local Safeway. An authority of no less renown than the Reuters agency tried to prevent me from doing something stupid. On September 4, they released an article about a group of US Safeway employees who had filed a grievance with the National Labor Relations Board over a company policy requiring clerks to smile and personally acknowledge customers. Apparently more than a few guys had "misread friendliness for flirtation."

I ignored this advice (at my peril). About the time I found the gumption to ask her out, she disappeared, and so I took out an "I Saw You" ad in an alt-weekly newspaper. She saw the ad (it turned out that a friend of a friend of a friend knew her) and I got her phone number, but she was not enthralled with my technique. I didn't even get a pity date. It did, however, produce the song "(Super)market Girl" featuring the most intentionally banal lyrics of all time:

Verse

> Shopping used to be a chore
> how I loathed the grocery store
> I had the cart with the squeaky wheel
> until I met a clerk with sex appeal

Chorus

> You're my super g-g-girl
> in a super super w-w-world
> how can I f-f-forget
> my super super m-m-market

Verse

> We're an item
> in the nine-items or less.
> Every time that scanner beeps
> my heart skips a beat.

Chorus

Verse

> Air Miles are good and fine
> but I'm flying cloud nine
> my heart's in high gear
> with my employee of the year

Chorus

The Plantains disbanded in May of 1999, a few weeks before I moved to Toronto. It was a convenient excuse. Being in a band mostly involved lugging gear from one place to another, and getting paid very little for the privilege. Things had changed in three short years. The post-interesting post-rock of Tortoise, and the neutered punk, emo-stylings of Modest Mouse were now popular. Alternative was dead, boy bands were taking over, and Limp Bizkit was eagerly awaiting the opportunity to start a riot at Woodstock.

Worse, indie-rock was fading. Pavement, who had thrown down the gauntlet in 1991 with *Slanted and Enchanted*, were disintegrating. Bill Calahan, the Smog svengali who had bummed everybody out with the 1995 album *Wild Love*, suddenly got happy. Will Oldham changed names so often – Palace Brothers, Palace Music, Palace, Bonnie "Prince" Billy – that fans lost track or lost interest. A best-of album entitled *Gimme Indie-rock Volume One* was released on the K-Tel label. Yes, that K-Tel label.

Lou Barlow married Kathleen.

The indie-rock torch is still being carried by bands like Pedro the Lion, Luna, and Cat Power, but the latest thing the kids are listening to is a poppier variant of indie-rock called twee. It's a cute, silly version of sixties pop, with some Pong-like pings thrown in for good measure. Twee features willful amateurism, jangly guitars, and the worship of *Pet Sounds*. Instead of sex and drugs, these pantywaists prefer puppy love and Pez.

The kings and queen of twee are a band from Glasgow called Belle and Sebastian. Fey enough to make Oscar Wilde blush, these pop poofters can actually play their instruments and carry a tune. Layered with horns and strings, *The Boy With the Arab Strap* and *If You're Feeling Sinister* feature lush arrangements and great songwriting – but it's all a bit too quiet for my liking. Great indie-rock wasn't afraid to yell – "Foolish" by Superchunk featured the immortal "One good minute could last me the whole year." Twee is more of a throat-clearing "ahem." Take the Magnetic Fields, the brain-child of Stephin Merritt. In 1999 he created a three-CD ency-clopedia of sad and not-so-sad songs about *l'amour* called *69 Love Songs*. This box-set features great crooning and clever lyrics ("you're unboyfriendable" and "It's making me blue/Pantone 292"), but the careful, exquisite arrangements lack a certain passion.

Twee isn't *bad*, but it lacks Brute. If Mick Jagger screamed about not getting any satisfaction, and indie-rock was desire muted by mild apathy, then twee whispers its fragile unhap-piness to a cello accomaniment. To put it another way, indie-rockers leave their house; twee fans suffer from agoraphobia.

There is, of course, non indie-rock Sad Bastard music. Nick Drake was a melancholy folk singer who detailed his disloca-tion from the world. He could recite the proverbial phone book and make you weep. Drake died from an accidental overdose of anti-depressants in 1974, at age twenty-six – thus ensuring he wasn't alive to hear his song "Pink Moon" used in Volkswagen Cabrio television commercials.

Chris Isaak combines heart-wrenching vocals with heart-breaking lyrics. His song "Wicked Game" is a Sad Batard clas-sic (I did an acoustic version at the launch party for the final *Single Guy Zine*). He understands obsession, as demonstrated by his album *Forever Blue,* which featured thirteen songs about a single breakup. See also: Matthew Sweet and his amazingly aching, achingly beautiful, achingly ache-filled 1991 album *Girlfriend*.

Bands like My Bloody Valentine took a different route to Sad Bastard by creating music and melodies that were very atmospheric and appropriately moody. While lyrics and vocals are important, sometimes the sheer din and dint of the music is enough to make you want to moan pathetically. By no coincidence, most of these wispy, textured arias came from England. Examples include Ride (*Nowhere*), Curve ("Coast is Clear"), Mazzy Star ("Fade Into You"), Portishead ("Sour Times"), and Black Box Recorder (*England Made Me*). Finally, there's that small, nearly unknown band called Radiohead. Try "Lucky" or "Karma Police" or nearly anything else from *OK Computer* – an album that is sad and stark and lonely and almost as brilliant as Thom Yorke thinks it is. See also: "How to Disappear Completely," from *Kid A*.

"Tainted Love" by one-hit wonder Soft Cell is another Sad Bastard clasic; a song whose power is derived mainly from its lyrics. Other lyric-driven songs include "Love Will Tear Us Apart" by Joy Division (whose lead singer, Ian Curtis, committed suicide), and Johnny Cash's "Flushed From the Bathroom of Your Heart." Before the crowd in Folsom Prison he drolled, "Up the elevator of your future, I've been shafted."

Weird Al wrote "One More Minute," which contains the line, "I burned down the malt shop where we used to go/just because it reminds me of you." A nervous fellow named John Darnielle is the genius behind the Mountain Goats. He wrote "Orange Ball of Love" which is about (I kid you not) dating a secret service agent who wears a wiretap. "And I know you'll be turning me in/but I also know your real name's not Amy Lynn." And finally, there is the Mr. T Experience, whose ditty "Even Hitler Had a Girlfriend" is the saddest song I've ever seen performed live.

The FBI tried to drive Noriega and David Koresh from their respective compounds by blasting terrible music (i.e., "These Boots Are Made For Walking" by Nancy Sinatra). Sad Bastard music often keeps the listener paralyzed with unhappiness, preventing him from leaving his bunker. There is the Woe is Me Plea, popularized by the Stone Roses and their song "I Wanna Be Adored." The chorus says it all, "I wanna, I wanna, I wanna be adored. I wanna, I wanna, I wanna be adored. I wanna, I wanna, I wanna be adored. I wanna, I wanna, I *gotta* be adored." Beck has a great wallowing song on *Mutations* entitled "Nobody's Fault But My Own." Canadian folkie Hayden hits the mark with "Hardly" (in which he gets his friend Lorraine to give his number to a woman in a coffee bar) and the *Moving Careful* EP.

Further woe can be found in R.E.M.'s "The One I Love," Damien Jurado's "Treasures of Gold," the naïveté of Built to Spill (*There's Nothing Wrong With Love*), the tiny, frightened tone of Sebadoh's "Spoiled," and "Come as You Are," by Nirvana (whose lead singer also killed himself).

Elliott Smith is a master of the Hurts So Good genre, which also includes Jonny Polonsky ("Scurvy Love'), Screaming Trees ("I Nearly Lost You") and the mumbled, Hurts So Bad despair of Arab Strap (*The Red Thread*). Nine Inch Nails cornered the aggressively depressed market and Nick Cave is an expert in dramatic discomfort. Finally, the Smiths and Morrissey's solo career are the Rosetta Stone of Sad Bastard. As friend and Plantain bass player Darren Gawle once noted in *Single Guy Zine*, "Morrissey has the eerie ability to speak for everyone who's ever watched the someone they fancy end up dating a complete prick."

There is classic Sad Bastard, including *In the Wee Small Hours* by Frank Sinatra, "Solitary Man" by Neil Diamond,

"Back of a Car" by Big Star, "Bookends Theme" and "For Emily, Whenever I May Find Her" by Simon and Garfunkel, and most of the back catalogue of Roy Orbison, Leonard Cohen, and Chet Baker.

A few gals have created Sad Bastard tunes for the single guy. Lisa Germano wrote a gem called "Geek the Girl." Juliana Hatfield used to be popular with single guys, but in retrospect, it's probably because she was cute – her music hasn't aged well. Thankfully, PJ Harvey (*Rid of Me*), Hole (*Live Through This*), Sleator-Kinney (*Dig Me Out*) and the Breeders ("Do You Love Me Now?") remain relevant. And then there's the queen of indie-rock, Liz Phair. On her landmark album *Exile in Guyville* she convinced single guys that women like her wanted, "all that stupid old shit/like letters and sodas." She yearned for a boyfriend, and I thought, "That's me!" She wasn't afraid to sing dirty words, or describe her habit of putting unmarried lips where they don't belong. Things quickly went downhill after she got hitched, however, and her next two albums suffered greatly.

It isn't all about wallowing, however. Certain kinds of Sad Bastard music are designed to inform the world that "I'm over you." Tobin Sprout, a former member of Guided by Voices, recorded the self-explanatory "Get Out of My Throat" for his 1997 album *Moonflower Plastic*. Hüsker Dü wrote "Never Talking To You Again." Years after Hüsker Dü disappeared, guitarist Bob Mould wrote the wonderful "Can't Fight It" for the *No Alternative* compilation album. The song is more resignation ("You're gone and I can't fight it") than celebration, but it got me through some rough times. Completing the Bob triumvirate is "A Good Idea" by Sugar – a classic love song about a guy who drowns his girlfriend in a river.

Finally, no serious discussion of popular music would be

complete without mentioning "I'm Not Your Stepping Stone," by the Monkees.

Few realize that how you listen to music is nearly as important as the music itself. I used to think I was the only guy who listened to the same sad song over and over and over again. It wasn't until the Spring of 1999, when my neighbor, Mr. X, went through a particularly nasty breakup, that I discovered other men acted as I did. For Mr. X, the song was "Wave of Mutilation" (UK Surf Mix) by the Pixies from the *Pump Up the Volume* soundtrack. An excellent choice on his part. The guitar track sounds as if it were recorded underwater, and the song morosely chugs along, with lyrics like, "Cease to resist, giving my goodbye/drive my car into the ocean."

For those unfamiliar with obsessive-compulsive behavior of the aural variety, the idea is to allow the melody to anesthetize you into a stupor in order to help you get through the day. The song becomes a four-minute koan to meditate upon. The trick is to not use the auto-repeat function of your CD player. The reason for this rule is somewhat unclear, but there is something soothing about having to hit the replay button every three or four minutes, for three or four days in a row. Perhaps it serves as a reminder that you're still alive.

The appeal of Sad Bastard music is that someone, somewhere, sometime, somehow, has written a song that perfectly describes your emotional chasm. Not only does this legitimize your pain, it saves you the trouble of trying to immortalize it. This leaves you more time to focus on more important things, such as arranging your record collection autobiographically.

STUCK IN SECOND GEAR: FRIENDS

Single guys might appear to lack knowledge of female consanguinity, but there is one particular arrangement that we are very familiar with: the platonic relationship. It is Latin for "charming but homely." Curiously, platonic rhymes with moronic.

The best way to understand the platonic relationship is to look at the race to split the atom during World War II. It took the biggest and brightest scientific minds studying the problem year after year to discover that plutonium will not react without heavy water and a hell of a lot of money. Much the same can be said for the platonic relationship if you substitute heavy water with alcohol (in copious amounts), and a hell of a lot of money with a *hell* of *a lot* of money.

The word "friends" can appear at the start of a relationship, thereby killing the dream, or at the end, after a woman dumps you. Being friends with a woman after being sent down to the minor leagues is the social equivalent of Buckley's Cough Mixture.

It tastes awful. And it –

I forget the rest of the slogan.

When a woman uses the word "friend" at the conclusion of date number one, most Astute Brutes smile and nod. They then furtively search for a shovel to dig a hole suitable for curling up and dying in. Most women fail to realize that the word "friends" does not prevent bruising upon impact. It's a crappy consolation prize. It's similar to the fallacy of saying that you came third in a race with two other contestants. You're not third, you're last.

Dead last.

I speak for most men when I implore women to substitute the f-word with the other, baser, and more infamous f-verb and the adverb "off." It is advantageous to both parties:

> » it's easy to memorize
> » it will save considerable heartache
> » it's a sentence that does not contain the word "friend"

The truth hurts for a little while. A lie hurts forever.

A variant on the "friends" miscommunique is the pre-emptive friendship (PEF). The PEF is a parasitic manoeuver initiated by the male, who ingratiates himself with a woman through befriendship, or the more technically correct "pseudo-befriendship." The ideal love forecast calls for strictly honorable intentions in the morning, moving to partly cloudy intentions with chance of precipitation in the afternoon, before moving into a heavy storm warning with lusts of up to fifty miles per hour beginning at dusk and continuing 'til the break of dawn.

In many cases, the female recipient of a PEF is a woman who's currently involved in a relationship, with the single guy's countervailing logic being: "She'll eventually realize the guy she's with is a clod, dump his ass, and I'll be there to snatch the rebound."

Such thinking results in DEFCON 2 levels of sexual tension for the male and absolutely no troubling side effects for the woman. The actual likelihood of such a scenario working out is exceedingly rare: .0000000001 percent with a margin of error of plus or minus .0000000001 percent. Prolonging this hamster wheel of insanity is the fact that most pathetic single men respond to the slightest sign of affection, and therefore deduce with glacial speed that the girl of their dreams is not, in fact, thinking about watching the Weather Channel.

What is preventing single guys from moving past the PEF is that unfortunately, every once in a while, friends become boyfriends – a mysterious transformation, like a caterpillar becoming a butterfly. Friends *can* mean "maybe later," if you do it right. However, women can take up to two years to decide, and reserve judicious use of the forever clause. Chances are, you won't molt into a boyfriend.

After being exposed to the apparently illogical mating rituals of women, single guys have no choice but to conclude that most women prefer jerks. Unlike most things involving women, there is a logical explanation for this particular phenom – anyone other than *you* standing beside the woman of your dreams is, obviously, a jerk. (Boyfriends are more commonly known as zombies: a 150-pound appendage that dangles uselessly off the arm of your lust object. So named because he's obviously eating her brain – why else would a smart, charming woman continue dating such a hideous monster?)

Unfortunately, being designated a friend changes everything. The man – who undoubtedly enjoyed spending time with his future wife until informed of the non-consummation clause – suddenly feels stupid for not figuring things out sooner and tries to disappear. Astute Brutes need to be more Machiavellian. The right thing to do is to stick around and prove you actually enjoyed her company, even if your interest was predicated on eventually receiving some naked company. While difficult, the man should continue the friendship just long enough to get the inside scoop on which of her friends are available and interested.

Before you dames finish dipping sharpened spears into curare over the friends thing, allow me to pontificate further.

Learning to live in peaceful co-existence with the occasional evil temptress or two is a worthwhile exercise. It develops much needed maturity and gives the man an opportunity to try and figure out How Women Think and What Women Want. Guys used to learn these things from their female siblings, but the trend towards smaller families has robbed us of such tutoring. Many single guys are only-children, myself included. We've never had a sister who tied up the phone line, hogged the bathroom, or played doctor with us. Without this inside track to understanding feminine wiles, their mystique has been revealed slowly, if at all.

As noted earlier, from August 1997 until May 1999 I had a female roommate (the one I had a temporary tattoo-like crush upon). She graciously became a surrogate sibling. She hogged the bathroom, tied up the phone line (usually around my neck), and any overtures of "physician and patient" would have resulted in her kicking my ass like a real big sister.

Don't get the wrong impression. We're not slimy, opportunistic bastards. A few us are scaly, opportunistic bastards. But most of us are charming men that you'd be happy to bring home to mother.

Provided, of course, that your mom isn't divorced or widowed.

ESCAPE PLANS

single guys on the lam

ROLE MODELS

The most common ways to meet women are often antithetical to the skill set of the Astute Brute. The meet-market is a perfect example. I am not a big fan of the clubbing scene because it's difficult to be witty, charming, and urbane when you're screaming to be heard over the throbbing bass. Dance clubs and bars remind me of English football – over ninety minutes of twenty-two guys shuffling their feet, bumping into each other, jostling for position, and looking for their moment of glory, only to end up not scoring ninety-eight percent of the time.

The Clubs have good intentions; they ooze alcohol, and the dim lighting and smoke machines make the inhabitants appear attractive. But these venues assume that entropy will equal ecstasy, while most single guys are content to experiment with inertia. I find it ironic that many clubs, usually on '80s nights, play the unofficial single guy anthem ("How Soon Is Now" by the Smiths). In this seven-minute dirge, the Mozzer hints that true love lurks in the nightclubs, before stating the awful truth:

> So you go and you stand on your own
> and you leave on your own,
> and you go home and you cry and you want to die.

Either we need our own Astute Brute nightclubs (featuring debating salons and smart drinks) or we need to learn to emulate big bears with claws and fangs if we want to catch Goldilocks. To help augment our grizzlyness, here are some men who've got the game all figured out.

My tall, blond, male Vancouver roommate (let's call him "Spiff"), who I first met in university in 1995, is the embodiment of the *How to Pick Up Girls!* philosophy. A smooth operator. An ur-Brute. A Lothario. Just a gigolo.

As you might expect, I studied him. I took notes. I crammed. Unfortunately, living with a player only teaches you how to become a player. It does not teach you how to find a girlfriend. Or, for that matter, how to act like a boyfriend. After apprenticing under a master craftsman, I discovered the "knack" or "Kavorka" is non-transferable. Spiff could make a pickup line like "Gee, your hair smells terrific" work.

How? It's sort of like rock lyrics. Most are terrible, but if sung with conviction (coupled with a wicked guitar riff, dude), the listener skips past the flaws. Thus, when the Scorpions sing, "Here I am. Rock you like a hurricane," we pump our fist and bang our head. If R.E.M.'s Michael Stipe were to sing the same lyric, we would guffaw.

Spiff was fearless when it came to asking women out. If they said no, it was their loss. He also had perseverance – forty seconds later, he was ready to try again. I lack the emotional calluses to deal with rejection quite so nonchalantly.

Thankfully, Spiff did manage to impart an invaluable tip: always get the woman's phone number. Sadie Hawkins is a terrible myth. As modern and as "with it" as most women are, ninety-nine percent of them will not call you back, even if they really, really, really like you. The reasons for this will remain forever unclear, but if you only take away one thing from reading this chapter, nay this book, ALWAYS GET HER NUMBER. This is the $E = MC^2$ of success with women.

In terms of Astuteness, Spiff was a Very Bad Good Boy. He was incredibly self-aware, and had developed his own unique interpretation of morality. He wasn't exactly a cautious pig, but he prefaced his worst comments with the phrase, "I hate to be a guy, but. . . ."

His Bruteness drank Brute 33 for breakfast. He used a real razor, he was good at billiards, he read *Maxim*, he was untidy, he could date strippers without panicking, and he ate steaks the size of your head. His only nod to feminism was a Lady Kenmore washing machine. When he wasn't bartending, he was clubbing or watching movies. He skied in winter and re-laxed at a nude beach during the summer. His life resembled a Club Med vacation, and I know people who would have paid a grand a week to live as he did. Still, being a player is hard work.

In the mid-eighties, psychologist Howard Gardner wrote *Frames of Mind*, which postulated a theory of multiple intelli-gences. Gardner believed that there were seven different in-telligences. For example, a ballet dancer has bodily-kines-thetic intelligence. Don't agree? Try doing a pirouette. Feel stupid? Exactly.

There is little doubt that Spiff possessed a very well-de-veloped interpersonal intelligence. He couldn't see dead peo-ple, but he could predict the likelihood of any couple he knew staying together. Part of interpersonal intelligence is instinct, part is experience. Spiff could correctly interpret motivations, detect the whispers of body language, and think on his feet. It's easy to dismiss Spiff's ability to read people like airport fic-tion, but his talents were rarified.

Spiff enjoyed the psychology of the hunt and the mental gymnastics nearly as much as the other kind of gymnastics. Intelligence involves problem solving, and my roommate had developed a path, a plan, a route, and a Venn diagram that calculated the probability of success in any given situation. Some of things he did seemed so obvious they wouldn't work. But they did. His biggest trick was introducing sexual undertones into conversations early and often. I'm not sure of the exact psychological mechanism, but get a woman thinking about sex, and eventually, she'll start thinking about having sex with the thought-provoking guy.

A zinester named R. Eirik Ott champions the Wussy Boy – a Nice Guy caught somewhere between guy and gay. Wussy Boy patron saints include Matthew Broderick and John Cusack. These fellows are outwardly sensitive, but inwardly tough. Like Dull Men, the Wussy Boy is aware of and content with his masculine limitations.

In the film *Say Anything*, John Cusack plays a kind-hearted kick boxer who manages to snag a date with class valedictorian Diane Court (Ione Skye). Cusack takes her to a graduation party where, eventually, classmate Mike Cameron asks the question on everyone's lips: how did the decidedly average Cusack manage to get the beautiful, overachieving Diane to go out with him?

> Cusack: I called her up.
> Mike: But how come it worked? I mean, what are you?
> Cusack: I'm Lloyd Dobler.

As a mantra, "I'm Lloyd Dobler" isn't quite "Calm blue ocean" or "You're in a forest with Heather Locklear," but it'll do. The next time you're thinking about thinking about not calling that special someone, simply tell yourself: I'm [insert your name]. By joining the cult of Cusack, we will remove the engrams – implanted by the galactic Emperor Xenu – that are preventing us from calling her, thus reaching a more enlightened state of Dobler-osity.

We really have lots to learn from Cusack. One of his recent films, *High Fidelity*, is about a single guy who views life through a music filter. Now that I think about it, that seems a little familiar. Perhaps I'm onto something here....

Aquinas. Montesquieu. Dex.

Summa Theologica. The Spirit of the Laws. The Tao of Steve. Philosopher Dex (Donal Logue) is the star of this indie film. He's a marijuana afficionado, he has a big gut, and lacks a discernable career trajectory. But he has hot and cold running chicks.

According to Dex, you're either a Steve (McGarrett, Austin, McQueen), or a Stu (Gomer Pyle, Barney Fife). The mythic Steve is a prototypical cool guy who, as the cliché goes, plays by his own rules. Steveness is a state of mind and a lifestyle. Stuness requires no further elaboration. The Tao of Steve is simple:

> *Eliminate your desire.*
> *Do something excellent in her presence.*
> *Retreat.*

The first is obvious – women like men who have more than one thing on their minds. The second rule is meant to prove your sexual worthiness. The third involves the idea that "we pursue that which retreats from us." More commonly known as playing hard to get.

I can't say that Spiff used an identical formula, but I would say that the Tao of Steve works like *How to Pick Up Girls!* works. If you have a system, and you stick to it faithfully, you'll eventually succeed. It's sort of like hitchhiking – stand by the side of the road with your thumb out, and eventually someone will pick you up. The great thing about using this method is that if a woman turns you down, you blame the system, not yourself. If it doesn't work, it just means that you need more practice. Think of it as a little insulation between you and them.

The only problem is that when Dex falls in love, Steveness becomes a liability instead of an asset. Like an ex-car thief, Dex finds it difficult to not jimmy a lock one last time.

Once again, it's the *Fight Club* dichotomy of Tyler and Joe – it takes one kind of fellow to snare a woman, and it takes a completely different kind of fellow to make a long-term relationship successful. Integrating the Brute and the Astute is difficult but crucial. At first blush, being Brute feels counter-intuitive, but it's like padding a resumé or being selective with the truth during a job interview. Everyone does it; if you can't manage a simulacrum of Brutishness, someone else will get hired.

(IM)PERSONALS

I have every confidence personal ads were once a very useful service, back when the population at large was honest. By my calculations, this last occurred during the Egyptian era:

> This SWM has found happiness in slavery! When he's not lifting 3,000-pound stone blocks for the Pharaoh's latest pyramid scheme, he enjoys smoking papyrus reed, making gold jewelry, and grave robbing. Drop him a scroll at Box #1.

Personal ads, unlike wine and Sherwood Schwartz sitcoms, have not improved with age. Sometime in the mid-eighties, everyone using the personal services decided to conform to an unwritten code that dictated a complete lack of imagination. This trend continues to the present, leaving us to carefully consider whether we seek "someone special" or instead prefer that "special someone."

The introduction of voice personals only worsened matters. In the old days, you would have to write a letter to the post office box listed in the personal ad. The person would write you back (hopefully). And so on and so on. (Remember, this was pre e-mail.) Writing letters requires a certain ability with language since not everyone can correctly use words like susurration, lugubrious, or antidisestablishmentarianism. The penpal routine acted as a kind of IQ test.

Voice personals are not Mensa stomping grounds. Back in the early 1990s, when I was in college, in student government,

I decided to sit in my office and listen to hour after hour of free voice personals. (Before you get outraged, I was merely investigating the truthfulness of the slogan "Power corrupts, absolute power corrupts absolutely.") I came to the conclusion that voice personals were only one neon-green aerobic step above chatlines in terms of intellectual evolution. Many people recording voice personals sounded as if they'd mastered the intricate nuances of telecommunication only a few minutes previous.

Ironically, a college education is required to decipher these rudimentary messages, filled as they are with subtext and semiotics. Here, then, is an attempt to tease out the logic (or lack therein) of a prototypical voice mail plea:

> Hi, my name is Mindy. I have long blonde hair and blue eyes. My friends say I'm attractive.

This is the most common tautology in the world of personals. Any friend that would dare suggest you're ugly isn't your friend. Hence, it is a completely useless phrase.

> I like to try new things.

Many people claim to appreciate novelty, few mean it. I have a restraining order to prove it.

> I'm a social drinker.

A classic hedge. No one brags about being a teetotaler, nor takes pride in getting blotto alone on Friday nights watching *Hee-Haw*.

> I'm looking for someone who's outgoing, humorous and interesting, fun to be with, and spontaneous.

Being anti-spontaneous is like being anti-world peace. Despite paying lip service to the unpredictable, many people have a better chance of experiencing spontaneous human combustion. As for the other traits, well, four-fifths of the general population believe they are those things.

> I'm not into head games.

That's a shame.

> So if you're interested, leave a message in Box 4761.

Caveat emptor.

The final evolution of the personal ad was made possible by the Internet. For the first time in history, sites like Swoon.com (sadly, deceased) and Nerve.com offered single guys the opportunity to find The Most Fantastic Woman in the Whole Wide World Web. Regardless of geography, regardless of time zone, you could potentially find your one true love. Swoon.com wasn't such a bad idea, really. Unlike twenty-five-words-or-less personal ads, Swoon.com asked you plenty of pertinent cultural questions and gave you enough space to express oneself fairly accurately.

Swoon.com worked as a database, allowing you to search for the specific qualities you desired (i.e., a college-educated, non-smoking, twenty-five-year-old Christian with brown eyes).

This allowed for the elimination of obvious idiosyncrasies. For those who enjoyed experimenting with various dream and nightmare scenarios, Swoon.com took on the feel of those workplace life-insurance policies. The more perverse permutations (a six-foot-plus acrotomophile who enjoys mini-golf) were identical to calculating disability payouts ("If I lose an ear *and* a big toe, I get $25,000").

Best of all, if the women of Swoon.com were unable to appreciate your unique charms, you needed only to redirect your browser to WomenBehindBars.com, whose denizens were all-too-eager to meet anyone at all. Even you.

Meeting women via the Internet is the perfect method for discovering how much putridness you're capable of emitting. Like penpals before it, an e-mail romance works best when you don't go and ruin it all by saying something stupid like, "Let's meet in person." Besides the natural inclination to lie about your appearance, it's easy to appear charming and confident in ASCII text, since you have hours or days to prepare a response.

Suppose you have a lot in common and you e-communicate well. You decide to rendezvous over coffee and realize that as important as personality might be, you cannot get past her goiter. You must then deal with the terrible realization that you are the detritus of humanity.

I've skipped over chatrooms because I dislike the whole concept. I have never bothered trying one. This might sound narrow-minded, but from what I've read, the odds are good I'll end up chatting with a German shepherd, a cop pretending to be a twelve-year-old girl, or a mixture of the two.

The other reason I'm not enamoured with chatrooms is

that I've been there and done that with something called a BBS. Short for Bulletin Board System, it was what nerds used before the Internet sold out. Each BBS was hosted on a separate computer, and you had to connect modem-à-modem. Once there, you had a text-only, rudimentary version of the modern webpage. You could post messages, chat with the SysOp (the system operator), play online ANSI games, and download "shareware." There were a few BBSs that allowed multiple users to connect simultaneously, and because most people visited BBSs in their city, neat little communities of people who disliked sunlight were formed.

During my days as a software pirate, I used a 2400 Baud modem. Compared to a 56K modem,

it

[pause]

was

[pause]

very,

[pause]

very,

[pause]

[pause]

slow.

After a few years of the BBS thing, my interest in talking to faceless individuals was exhausted. I still love e-mail, but having tried newsgroups and mailing lists and such, I realize I'm still a people person. Given the anonymity of the Internet, it's far too easy for cyberspace to become cipherspace.

I LEFT MY HEART IN NEW YORK: BLIND DATES

Ah, the blind date, a risky adventure, similar to Russian Roulette – except that if things go badly, you'll still be alive to regret the experience. Or maybe it's more like a liver transplant – a difficult operation that often results in organ rejection. As the television show of the same name has proven, the blind date can be horrific. Mating ritual bloopers provide endless fascination for those who do not partake in the experience directly, much like snuff films.

For those who have yet to see this syndicated masterpiece, *Blind Date* sets up two people, with cameras documenting their every move. During the show, little thought balloons created by the show's staff appear – similar to those on *Pop Up Video*. These doodles contain mostly snarky comments about the participants.

The show isn't always must-see TV, but at its best, nothing beats the discomfort captured when the two participants simply aren't working out. A bad *Blind Date* is like undergoing surgery without an anesthetic. Or an autopsy performed on a still-wriggling cadaver.

It purports to be reality television, but I'm certain clever editing plays a role in the final product. (Besides, single guys use entertainment to escape from reality, since we receive transmissions from the Failure Channel every morning, courtesy of the Bathroom Mirror Network.) As an ongoing sociology experiment, it's not without validity. *Blind Date* has pioneered a new concept in television dating shows by combining the *cinema verité* of Godard's *Breathless* with the brutality of *Cops*. Previously, the boondoggle has always occurred off camera, a tradition dating back to 1965, when *The Dating Game* premiered. Having the participants describe the date creates a "he said/she said" dynamic, whereas *Blind Date* allows the viewer to trace the chalk outline for themselves.

I can't recommend appearing on the show, but single guys should consider preserving their dating embarrassments with a concealed video camera. Recording the event for posterity will allow guys to analyze their mistakes (and successes). In the wannabe mockumentary *Twenty Dates,* an annoying guy (Myles Berkowitz) films his female encounters and manages to find the woman of his dreams in the process. Not everything in the film is true, but it shows the value of being able to pinpoint problems through instant reply or slow-motion.

Blind Date documents the most terrifying type of vision impairment, the "double-blind" experiment. This myopic situation occurs when neither party have previously met. Dick and Jane gather at a certain place, at a certain time, and stare at one another to see who blinks first. These encounters are rare.

The short-sighted affair known as the "semi-double blind date" occurs when friends common to both parties are present. The most common format is when an established "couple" introduces two pathetic single friends in the hopes that rubbing shoulders will generate static cling. The couple act as moderators (or worse, mediators) trying to initiate conversations, or keep them on the tracks.

These outings often foster a tense, hostage/negotiator atmosphere, combining the comfort of an inaugural skydive with the time constraints of an SAT. Two people who normally might have had a decent relationship collapse under the pressure of super human scrutiny. These fiascoes are similar to what happens when well-intentioned zoologists force pandas to mate in captivity. Doing anything romantic with gawkers present is extra pressure we don't need.

If the semi-double blind date is successful, the romantic life-support provided by your mutual friends is often a bad thing. Behind-the-scenes assistance ("she loves Thai food") usually results in love with training wheels. Once removed, things get wobbly.

Finally, there is the ambush known as the "set-up." This provides no early warning. A well-meaning couple sticks two people – who are perfect for each other – alone in a room so they can immediately start proving their friends wrong.

I might seem overly critical of blind dates, but it's a case of do as I say, not as I do. In the fall of 1998, I was getting desperate about my women problems (the problem being, there weren't any). I realized that my lack of persistence and courage was at fault. Clearly, I needed to take some chances and do some-thing genuinely spontaneous and impulsive, instead of think-ing so damn much. If I didn't do something soon, I would drown in a tsunami of regret and bitterness. And so, in September of 1998, I flew to New York for a blind date.

As Dave Barry likes to say: "I am not making this up."

The whole mess began when I faxed an article to *Details* magazine. I might hate their philosophy, but I revere their payment schedule. An intern named Jezebel (name changed for easy laugh) read my story (about going to a party at Douglas Coupland's house), and decided to visit my website. After viewing the Win-A-Date with Ryan contest, she decided to fax off an entry. (To prove I learn from my mistakes I'm omitting the URL.) She invited me to visit, offered me a place to stay (her apartment!), and procured two tickets to a concert featuring Canadian alt-rock band Sloan.

My initial reaction was to politely decline, but my friends thought this was the impulsive kick-start my achy, breaky heart so desperately required. Playing the "what if" game soon became a favorite pastime. My blonde female roommate helped convince me by repeatedly chanting, "You have to go." My heartstrings were also tickled by the pronouncement of those four most romantic words, "Air Canada Seat Sale."

A final, mitigating factor was Jezebel's self-description: "a healthy mix of Elisabeth Shue (face), Diane Keaton (mannerisms), and Elle MacPherson (body)." What red-blooded guy wouldn't be excited by the prospect of zingy, Diane Keatonish banter?

An e-mail and a few phone calls with Jezebel helped convince me that I was stupid and randy enough to star in an adaptation of *Sleepless in Seattle*. Besides, by making the mistake of consulting with my friends, the trip had taken on a life of its own. At a certain point in the process, a blind date, any blind date – but especially one that involves flying to NY – becomes less about you and more about your friends wanting to live vicariously through you.

Less than a week after receiving her fax, I was on a plane headed towards La Guardia Airport. A taxi soon deposited me at *Details* headquarters – the closest we could get to the top of the Empire State Building at sundown. Scared, tired, and scared, I tapped into hitherto unknown sources of adrenaline, strode onto the elevator and pressed the button marked "destiny."

First impressions suck, and despite the impeccably refreshing red-eye flight from Vancouver, I perhaps could have done slightly more to ease the awkwardness of the opening gambit (i.e., roses or chocolates). Conversations were a bit of a problem. There were none. Despite commonalties – similar tastes in music, we were both Canadian, we both exhaled CO_2 – there wasn't enough adhesive to make us bond, either spiritually or biblically. We were actors in a foreign film speaking terribly translated subtitles. ("I love you poorly. I am damn unsatisfied to be dating in this way. Beware the grenade of romance.")

A telling moment during our first evening excursion occurred as we stared at the bar's television, watching a sporting event neither of us were interested in, willing it to transform into a teleprompter. The chemistry was lacking. She seemed playful on the phone but was withdrawn in person, which didn't help matters. Perhaps the idea of me flying out to New York was slightly more exciting than the actual event. Anticipation, they say, is the best part.

It would later emerge that she liked thin guys – emaciated heroin addicts, for example – which I unfortunately do not resemble. This preference is justified revenge for the male fixation with attractive anorexics like Calista Flockhart. Since I'm neither ecto- nor endomorph, I calmly accepted this rebuffing. I will, however, say this: I know Elle MacPherson. Elle MacPherson is a friend of mine. Jezebel, you're no Elle MacPherson.

I should have flown out for the weekend, but I got greedy. A week-long blind date had sounded enticing – clearly it was fate that put my fax in her hands. This was to be a meeting of soulmates. Meetings behind closed doors. Frequent meetings. Instead of a dapper Tom Hanks, I was becoming the weepy

Meg Ryan (no relation). Meanwhile, my date more closely resembled a tough-as-nails hero that once dumped a man just to watch him cry.

When you rent a bad movie, you simply return it. If you feel particularly vindictive, you might decide to be unkind and not rewind. But humans are a slightly different matter (especially those who travel 4,000 kilometres on a whim) and I assumed that my host would put me up, even if she couldn't put up with me. Wrong. Jezebel informed me that the guest room, like my heart, had to be empty by Monday. At this point, the "Sleepless" part became a poignant, if not prescient, description of my adventures.

Eventually, I decided to take the Monday evening Greyhound to Toronto (my ticket was Vancouver-Toronto-New York) and fly home a few days later. The twelve-hour bus ride gave me time to reflect. "Why?" became a recurring leitmotif, which I eventually began chanting aloud – repeatedly. No one paid me any attention since, after all, it was Greyhound.

Despite my bitter tone – a byproduct of being treated like a worm in the Big Apple – I didn't have a completely terrible time. I have few regrets about the experience. I now realize it's better to have done something and be temporarily disappointed, than torture yourself endlessly with the possibilities. And I learned some things. Firstly, blind date sequels will not be filmed on foreign soil, ensuring that my rejections will be far more rapid, convenient, and most importantly, cost effective. Secondly, taking some chances and following your dreams isn't always such a bad idea. While reviewing my diary for this chapter, I was surprised at how much bemusement and how little depression I experienced. Psychologists, of course, have a term for this particular brand of nostalgia.

Denial.

MY HOMEWORK WAS
NEVER QUITE LIKE THIS:
HIGH SCHOOL

In a recent article about the future, Ominous magazine predicted that by the year 2525, there will be a pill that eliminates romance-induced heartburn. This will be the first such drug without a bitter almond aftertaste. *Ominous* also predicts that by the year 3535, America will elect its first female president. Her inaugural piece of legislation will involve pairing men and women off at birth, creating a utopic world free from the taint of awkward first dates and disastrous expressions of free will.

Until then, solving the problem of meeting women remains. The most popular ideas still involve enticing men and women to the same place at the same time. Theoretically, this sounds plausible – B.F. Skinner serenaded male and female rats with Sinatra 78s to good effect – the problem is that too many real-life variables disrupt the process. Reaction to my person-sized Skinner box – featuring operant conditioning through electric shocks and a risotto pellet dispenser – has been tepid.

Recently I discovered a superior solution to our courtship woes:

~~Giant robots.~~

High school for adults.

Given my selective memory, I remember high school as a simpler time – boys were made of snakes and snails and puppy dog tails, and girls were made of sugar and spice and other things nice. But like anything involving youth, it's wasted on the young. I'm not sure when my Norman-Rockwell-sipping-sodas revival might occur, so high school is the next best thing. Who wouldn't enjoy returning to the days of giggling and passing notes in homeroom and having Jennifer's friend Roma tell Kelli to tell you that Jennifer might like you?

Despite the increased likelihood of arriving at a final exam wearing only a pair of underwear, high school was a great environment for chasing girls. And I say this despite being voted Most Likely Not to Talk to an Attractive Woman.

You were guaranteed to see the same people day in and day out. If you were too scared to talk to your unrequited love in September, you had a whole year to procrastinate. Sock-hops, lunches in the cafeteria, and the occasional class together provided you with ample opportunity not to proposition her. High school was one non-stop escalator ride through a hormone hothouse, all leading towards the inevitable encounter when you watched, horrified, as someone else asked her to the prom five minutes before you were going to.

It's no coincidence that well-meaning advice columnists tell single people to enroll in continuing education classes. The problem is that night classes conducted in local community colleges or fetid elementary school gymnasiums fail to satisfactorily recreate the high school environment. Few find pottery, poetry, or puppetry appealing. University would be the ideal environment, were it not for the cost and the thinkin' involved.

My proposal combines high school with urban, modern, hipster studies. It would be the ideal dating club – a high school/college for single people that would exist solely for the purpose of meeting people in a relaxed atmosphere. Imagine classes like:

» Seinfeldian Philosophy 101: Neurosis and Narcissism
» TV Analysis 212: Socialist Overtones in *The Smurfs*
» Christian Allusions in Popular Culture 325:
  Jughead as Christ figure

I envision many things – limited enrolment, no fraternities, small class sizes, co-educational facilities to better facilitate co-habitation, no fraternities, and women's studies (with highly anticipated take-home projects). And a dress code consisting of school-girl uniforms with the knee-socks and the pleated skirts and the white dress shirts and the cute little black Mary Janes and the principal being reluctantly forced to administer punishment to delinquent girls in the privacy of his office while....

[Publisher's note: The next twelve paragraphs were removed and mailed to Penthouse Forum. *The adventures of Bambi, Candi, and Ryan will appear in the September issue. For the record, Ryan would like to note that "I couldn't believe it was happening to me."]*

SLAVING OVER A HOT DATE: COOKING FOR LOVE

If a return to the past isn't appealing, perhaps the present holds some answers. During a MuchMusic interview for the Zoo TV tour, a U2 member who wasn't Bono noted that Americans seem to think they don't exist until they appear on television. Because that little cathode ray tube holds so much power over our lives – having raised a substantial number of us – our existence isn't validated until we merge with a television, *Poltergeist*-style.

Since most women fail to acknowledge that I exist, I decided to try for my 415 degrees of fame on a Canadian game show called *Cooking for Love*. I have enough confidence (or is that stupidity?) to go on television and pretend that I know how to cook, yet I lack the courage to strike up a conversation with a woman who's sitting next to me at a bar. Reconcile my selective bravery and you'll truly, madly, and deeply understand me.

For those who haven't seen it, *Cooking for Love* is basically *The Dating Game* meets *Iron Chef*. While less ribald than the American shows that inspired it, *Cooking* retains a certain spice, due in large part to the crush-worthy hostess, Thea Andrews. She keeps things going as three men vie for the affections of a mystery woman by cooking a meal of her choosing (occasionally the genders reverse). There is no recipe provided, the meal is a secret until the show begins, and the participants are given but thirty minutes to shake and bake.

Thankfully, Canadian programmers aren't as interested in humiliating their contestants to ensure good ratings, mainly because they know it won't help – no one is watching. Besides, our *Charter of Rights and Freedoms* appears to protect us from questions like "If you were a vegetable, which one would you be and why?" Grilling contestants is frowned upon. Grilling food, fine.

Getting on the show involved coming to terms with that most chilling event: cattle call. This worried me, as I have a skin condition known as "inner beauty." My best feature is my intelligence, but that claim should be treated with grave skepticism, given my willingness to appear on a game show that involves a hot stove.

The audition meant going to the downtown YMCA one Saturday – would feats of strength be required? – and filling out a form that posed such searing questions as: "How often do you date?" (not often enough), "What statement would best describe your culinary know-how?" (I have graduated from instant noodles to vegetable curries), and "What is your daytime phone number?" I tried answering the questions as honestly as possible (416-KL5-1212), although I fudged a bit on occupation, purporting to be a business and technology writer to throw them off the journalistic scent.

I was then ushered into a small room to answer a few questions in front of a video camera. The handler asked me about my New York blind date. I answered. She laughed, snapped a Polaroid of me (clothed), and promised to let me know either way within two weeks.

Nearly a month later – long enough to imagine several scenarios involving laughter and the pitying shaking of heads – I got the call.

I was in.

Luckily, I had spent the intervening weeks primping and preening. I had bought a pair of contact lenses, got my hair cut, dyed the remainder blond, and revitalized my closet. I needed to bring "two to three camera-ready outfits" to the tap-ing, which meant no plaids, stripes, checkers, prints, white or red clothing, or jeans – a list that describes my wardrobe per-fectly. I enlisted my friend Rob who, while not gay, certainly knows his way around a clothes rack. A few hundred dollars later, we achieved what he dubbed "Biggemalian."

I spent most of the appointed Sunday cultivating an ulcer before arriving at the studio. The director walked us men folk through the soundstage, pointing out our marks (television talk for duct tape). Then we met host Thea Andrews.

It is the job of the author to create concise, vivid character-izations, so here goes: Thea Andrews is very, very, very pretty.

Some might find it counter-productive to have the host of the show be so drop-dead gorgeous, but to me, the logic is clear. If the male contestants can manage to appear more in-terested in the mystery girl than in Thea, the chances of infi-delity or even leering at other women are minimal.

Thea went over the forms we had filled out so long ago and tried to determine what we were all about. It would be easy to dismiss Thea if she weren't so pleasant, charming quick-witted, and intelligent. The contestants are free to act like bimbos or mimbos, but Thea radiates calm and cool. Did she make me nervous? Only momentarily. I relaxed appre-ciably once I realized that Thea Andrews is just another at-tractive woman I'm never going to sleep with.

Next, a producer named Jeni did her best to explain the fine line between PG-13 (good) and NC-17 (bad). For example, an entire episode had to be scrapped because a male chef said the word "dildo." Not only is that word too lascivious, but it was inappropriate given that the show is meant to eliminate the need for that particular appliance. Jeni also informed us that our mystery woman was "hot." When pressed, Jeni admitted she always said that, but then rushed to assure us that in this particular case, it was actually true.

All the while, we three chefs were supposed to be bonding. Ed (contestant #1) was a software consultant. He owned a house. Rob (contestant #3, and not to be confused with my clotheshorse buddy of the same name) was a manager at a telecommunications firm. He also owned a house. I am a writer. I have been inside a house.

Rob was the sort of fellow who clearly knew how to "party hard" and "get a little wild." He was also physically fit and confident, and might as well have had "winner" tattooed to his forehead. Ed had a nervous charm about him, amplified somewhat by the fact that he actually wanted to win. After our makeup was applied (sadly, there was no fluffer), the aprons went on, the gloves came off, and the cameras started rolling. Lucy, the mystery woman, announced that she wanted a couscous and grilled vegetable salad with an orange vinaigrette. This was precisely when I realized Lucy and I had no future together. I don't go in for that S&M stuff, and only a sadist would request a meal of such complexity.

My suspicions were confirmed when she claimed to enjoy ten-kilometer jogs.

As part of the research for my chef character, I had flipped through many cookbooks and thoughtfully considered the pictures. I also had consulted with a cook friend of mine who works at a Restaurant With Actual Ambiance (i.e., an expensive one). He advised me to make the food flavorful, to ensure it was presented tastefully, and most importantly, to marinate my slop with reckless abandon.

As we tossed our couscous about, Thea would periodically interrupt and get to know us better. The chefs each got to pose one question to the mystery girl. I asked, "What part of the bookstore would I find you in?" Lucy replied she was currently interested in *feng shui* and that she also liked trashy novels. Her apartment might be harmonious, but our debates about the relative merits of Danielle Steele and Haruki Murakami most likely wouldn't be.

The best way to a woman's heart might be through her stomach (provided the meal is low-carb), but like many men, all of my best meals have involved serving the same thing: a credit card to a waiter. And even if I were an Iron Chef whose cuisine reigned supreme, the mystery woman only has one bite of each meal to discern this. So instead of worrying about taste or edibility, I focused on presentation. I converted my eggplant circles and zucchini sticks into a smiley face, which earned the audience laughter it deserved.

Alas, I did not win. If *Cooking for Love* is the televisual equivalent of a personal ad – a nymphomercial? – then I clearly failed to sell the sizzle. But thankfully, the two leftover men are not forced to do the dishes, or worse, eat the meal they created. And continuing the standard of Canadian game show prize opulence set by *Definition* (where the winner would have his or her parking validated for free), we received a bottle of Inniskillin Riesling, two packs of gum, a mousepad, a Kitchenaid pamphlet, a spoon as wooden as my acting, and two condoms. Perhaps more importantly, I was allowed to leave with my dignity intact.

The media is blamed for the ills of society: school shootings, teenage pregnancies, those obsequious, rubber, singing fish. We rarely consider that television might provide the occasional solution to our quandaries. I'm not sure appearing on *Cooking* validated my existence (they certainly didn't validate my parking), it definitely didn't get me a date, but at least I now know why they call it the boob tube.

HE BLINDED HER WITH SCIENCE

If television can't help us, perhaps science holds some answers. The big innovation of the year 2000 was something called SpeedDating (SpeedDating.com). For twenty bucks, you got seven supersonic blind dates in forty-nine minutes. At the end of the night, you marked a dating card to indicate who you'd like to see again, and if the attraction was mutual, you received their phone number(s) within forty-eight hours.

The process was designed for busy Jewish singles (gentile versions are being organized) and appears to work quite well. Why waste a few hours on a blind date with some schmuck you instantly dislike?

SpeedDating is similar to an idea I've had for years: the Columbia Dating House. Imagine going out on any four dates for a penny, provided you select three more dates at regular Club prices.

If neither SpeedDating nor the Columbia Dating House appeals to you, there is always Speed Seduction. The brainchild of Ross Jeffries, Speed Seduction is the only evolution/devolution in makin' out since Eric Weber's *How to Pick Up Girls!*. In the early nineties, Jeffries wrote *How to Get the Women You Desire Into Bed: A Down and Dirty Guide to Dating and Seduction for the Man Who's Fed Up With Being Mr. Nice Guy*. Then, thinking better of forcing guys to waste time on dinner and a movie, he developed breakneck bewitchment. Utilizing the techniques of neurolinguistic programming (a method of communicating with the unconscious mind through language patterns), Jeffries will teach you how to impart lewd suggestions through a kind of subliminal hypnosis. By inserting words like penetrate and surrender, or mispronounced double entendres like "below me" (blow me), into your conversations, you increase your chances of getting her into bed in thirty minutes or less (or so). The actual science is shaky, but Speed Seduction is no better or worse than single guy phrases like: "But why not?" and "Pretty please?"

The only problem with Speed Anything is that it favors those who are good at first impressions. Some single guys will always remain allergic to women. Scientific attempts to find a female antihistamine are progressing slowly, refining trephination techniques is a major headache, and we're still waiting for Lamaze-like breathing exercises to help keep us calm when conversing with women. The best hope lies in systematic desensitization, a method of de-shying first envisioned by John B. Watson and refined by Joseph Wolpe. The therapy works by gradually acclimatizing the subject to the fear-eliciting stimuli.

For example, if the subject fears black widow spiders, a therapist would expose him to progressively more anxiety-invoking representations of creepy crawlies – spider photos to toy spiders to dead spiders to spiders at a zoo to finally touching a real live actual black widow spider.

This therapy has been attempted on single guys with limited success. Following the aforementioned progression, subjects have been exposed to photos of women, inflatable women, morgue women, and peep show women, before finally touching a real live actual woman. Still, most single guys get less anxious touching a venomous arachnid than a woman. These experiments haven't been a complete waste, however. Researchers discovered a significant proportion of single men no longer shun women who kill their partners after mating.

Women, meanwhile, are content to practic aversion therapy.

Science is happy to dither about trying to cure cancer, when the real glory lies in aphrodisiacs and royal jelly. The Bunsen burner and beaker set still think Love Potion #9 actually exists.

In the fall of 1999 I learned that a little cologne helps mask questionable personality traits. After mixed results with Old Spice, I finally settled on a scent called Of a Man, which has received favorable reviews. It's not wild boar sweat or 5-alpha-androst-16-er-3-one (a.k.a. androsterone) but a good odor can hide many a noxious habit. Sadly, this advantage dissolves when I tell people the name of the product. They're giggling at me, not with me.

Pheromones might be the Holy Grail we'll never discover. We need the genetic code that causes baby ducks to imprint with the first thing they see. Konrad Lorenz was the guy who figured this out, and we've probably all seen photos or film of a bunch of ducklings following Lorenz around as if he were Daffy. The scientific community has spent a lot of time and money on the Human Genome Project – let's ensure it does something useful.

A Swiss company named Skim.com recently created the sort of apparel only a single man – or a crypto-fascist – would truly appreciate. Each garment has a unique six digit mailbox code, visible to all, which acts as an e-mail address (i.e., 666999@skim.com). The garment owner receives an access code for their pants, or whatnot, so they can retrieve their messages and check out who checked them out.

It is infinitely easier to email someone from the safety of your home computer than to try to hit on them in person. As great as this might be, anything that makes our undertaxed Brute even more anemic isn't a good thing. Besides, the six digit tattoo isn't exactly sharing esteemed historical company.

With fashion, simpler is better; less is more. I recomment wearing lots of sweaters, mainly because a guy at a bus stop once told me that women still dig guys in sweaters.

PAY TO PLAY

Finally! All the really dirty stuff everyone was waiting to learn more about in the first place.

In free weekly newspapers that feature frequent grammatical errors, you'll find classified ads that feature pictures of attractive women who pepper their speech with exclamation points:

> Naughty, nasty girls! Live, 24 hours a day! 1-800-BAD-BABES. Girls who jaywalk! Girls who run with scissors!! Girls who swim right after a big meal!!! Have your wildest fantasies brought to life. $3.95 per minute.

These ads sound tempting. The worst-case scenario is an ear infection. These women, along with the gals on late-night television chatline commercials, are very eager to meet Mr. Right – a special kind of guy who has a valid credit card and knows how to use it. But when I was a kid, obscene phone calls were free, dammit.

Technology promised us automated sidewalks, flying cars, and Stepford Wives. Single guys are still waiting for any of the above, although the folks at RealDoll.com might disagree. "We use an exclusive formulation of ultra flesh-like silicone, which emulates the soft, elastic feel of human skin." RealDoll is flexible (she can withstand over three-hundred percent elongation), heat resistant (she can withstand temperatures that exceed 300 degrees), odorless, flavorless, not to mention stain and water resistant. You can choose from Leah, Stacy, Celine, Tami, Nika, Amanda, Stephanie, and Mai.

RealDoll lets you avoid the plastic hassle of inflatable women. If you're looking for a beautiful gal who caters to your whims without complaint, RealDoll.com is the answer – provided you have six grand to spare. Sorry boys, she's non-refundable. "RealDoll is very sturdy, but not meant to sustain extremely violent abuse. However, we stand behind our product and do whatever we can to satisfy our customers. In the unlikely event of a tear in the silicone flesh, you can easily repair the damage yourself with commercial grade silicone caulking, found at your local hardware store."

More romantic words have never been committed to parchment.

As I often overhear in the bathrooms of dive bars, "You don't buy beer, you rent it." Similarly, the company of certain women can be purchased in convenient half-hour increments. It's like a kissing booth, with a slightly different verb. For most single guys, hookers are a type of fishing lure. Approaching a woman is difficult enough without the potential of being arrested. Add the yucky disease factor, the illegality, the immorality, plus the cost, and the decision is a no-brainer.

I visited South Korea and Thailand in the spring of 1998 and spent a few days in Bangkok. Motivated purely by journalistic curiosity, I went to the most ridiculously named go-go bar I could find – Super Pussy. It was genuinely disconcerting to meet women who wanted to get to know me and my wallet in a very intimate manner. I was not tempted.

Honest.

If taxi meter maidens aren't your thing, perhaps you'd be

more comfortable brokering a matrimonial mortgage through a mail-order bride service. Many former Eastern Bloc women haven't been exposed to many feminist values – such as pride, backbone, or pioneering – and this appeals to some men. Conversely, Russian men are often described as unromantic, drunken louts – worse, there's not enough of them to go around.

I did some electronic ogling at LoveMe.com (a cross between eBabe and eBay), but I'm not convinced this is an appropriate solution. To me, the mail-order bride offers few benefits. Shipping and handling is not included. Allow six to eight weeks for delivery, add eight dollars extra for CODs, a seven percent tax applies to Michigan residents. Offer void where prohibited.

I fail to see how anyone would fall for such a scam. When I was eight, I mailed away for Sea Monkeys.

They turned out to be brine shrimp.

SINGLE GUYS

we need to talk

IT DOESN'T HAVE TO BE THE END OF THE WORLD

The unexamined life is not worth living, argued dead Greek philosopher Socrates. But I've come to realize that constant solipsism is a tad overrated. The Astute Brute is too clever by half – he can spot the flaws in religion, marriage and prostitution but has trouble creating viable alternatives. Besides, the rituals and permutations of the relationship circuit function passably for most people. When a certain type of guy continually slips through the cracks, we blame him, not the system.

So whose fault is it anyway? Tyler Durden shakes his bloodied fist at broken homes: "What you see at Fight Club is a generation of men raised by women." In *Stiffed*, Susan Faludi suggests that capitalism got us into this fine mess. And I blame ~~polygamy~~ postmodernism.

Despite my painfully normal, middle-class, two-parent upbringing, despite my outrageous belief that the free market might not be perfect, and despite my attempts at smashing the hall of mirrors, I'm still confused about how to be an integrated guy in a bipolar world. I'm not alone, so to speak. Scotchguarded by P.C., molded in the blast furnace of second-wave feminism, sculpted by the legislated nostalgia of the fifties, sixties, and seventies, the Astute Brute tribe is large. Taken singly – a Sad Bastard song here, a wistful movie there, a quirky zine hither, a poignant book thither – we don't appear very imposing. But combined, you get a nation of millions who have lost their way and deserve a compass.

The first step in A.A. is admitting you are powerless over

alcohol. I certainly haven't been shy about describing my romantic befuddlement – you could fill a book with what I don't
know about women. I've done my best to describe single guy
habits, patterns, and problems. The next step is generating solutions. Or getting blotto.

Medieval medicine was very crude (hacksaw amputations,
bloodletting, aromatherapy) and in a similar manner, most
single guys find the cure (blind dates, personal ads, the produce section of the grocery store) worse than the ailment. We
need a liminal space between the singles bar and sitting home
alone every Saturday night. According to *Girls!* author Eric
Weber, art galleries might be one answer: "Museums are fantastic places to pick up on chicks – especially if you dig the serious, intellectual type. When a girl gets picked up while ap-
preciating art, she somehow feels she hasn't really been
picked up."

The trick is finding situations where Astuteness is an asset,
not a liability. This is why single guys must pool their resources.
The mating game is very competitive, but only through cooper-
ation will things improve. We need romantic socialism:

Single guys of the world unite!
You have nothing to lose but your clothes.

Until "to each, according to his emotional neediness" becomes law, we must resign ourselves to the fact that few
methods of meeting women suit the Astute. Either we address
our inconsistent and misapplied Bruteness, or we invert the
paradigm and toss it outside the box. If *Maxim* is the voice of
unapologetic Brutes, then we must champion Astuteness with
an equal vigor. With the right buzz, aggressive Astuteness
could become the new Brute. Today, jocks kick sand in our
face; tomorrow, women will swoon as we complete the Sunday
New York Times crossword in pen. Moose, meanwhile, will sit

alone and ignored as he struggles with Jumble: That Scrambled Word Game.

Beyond promoting Astute, we need to take pride in being single. The more often we discuss our predicament, the more normalized "between relationships" will become. There is such a thing as a *very* late bloomer and history *can* be written by non-winners. The confirmed bachelor shows how single life can be stable, not transitional. Many respected scientists (Sir Isaac Newton), politicians (Ralph Nader), and famous authors (ahem) never marry, but this info gets buried under reams of Hallmark propaganda. Flying solo might be easier if we weren't constantly reminded – by Disney and Mom – that a single guy is like half a pair of scissors. We are forced to ignore bicycles built for two and Merchant Ivory films. The need to repress reality is what made the Very Lonely Planet possible – a fugue state of our own design.

Despite our stiff upper lip and clenched jaw muscles, some days are difficult, and even the automatic doors at the supermarket won't acknowledge our existence. Yet the single guy does not abandon ye hope upon entering the Very Lonely Planet. He perseveres, sometimes wrong-headedly, but like Sisyphus, he keeps giving that boulder a shove.

Constant striving for the great escape is admirable, but our mental prison *has* benefits. Sadly, single guys rarely take advantage of all that spare time, instead choosing to master *Tomb Raider* or assuaging their emotional void through the purchase of nifty, shiny, crap. Instead, why not learn a new language, run a marathon, compose a song about mollusks, publish a zine about salt, make a super-8 film about seagulls, write a book about hat-blocking. *Anything.*

The terrible truth is that there is a direct correlation between a lack of smurfing and a surfeit of Astute. In the absence of distracting girly molecules, we have the potential to reach near-genius levels of introspection. Curmudgeons have always been clear on this point; dramatist Philip Barry believes, "Love is two minds without a single thought." There are exceptions (Marie Curie and her husband Pierre) but have you ever met a dumb monk? Exactly.

To invoke a cliché, use your Very Lonely Planet vacation to "find yourself." It's okay to take an occasional female sabbatical – it's the difference between being intentionally and unintentionally single. No more worries about where that stray arm should go whilst spooning. No more endless hours dithering in the video store or battling between *The Bridges of Madison County* or *The Bridge on the River Kwai*.

Don't get me wrong, the removal of clothing and the tumbling and the noises and the hey-hey is great too. You guys know what I'm talking about – a trip to the laundromat. But occasionally, you have to take the time to carefully sort through your dirty laundry before you're ready for some bounce.

Meditation is best in moderation, however. Let the chattering of the monkey mind cease for a while, but remember that long-term singleness grinds grooves into ruts, making it even tougher to find and maintain a relationship. The trick to meeting someone is to not appear feverishly desperate, which is why you should immerse yourself in a worthwhile project. You're more likely to discover someone when you're not actively looking for them. So quit looking for love (in all the wrong places). Go ahead, give it a try.

Cut. That was terrible. Another take please, this time with feeling and verve. People, people, quiet on the set.

It was either Sartre or Count Chocula who believed that ulti-mately, we are alone in the universe. Keep this in mind the next time you see an attractive couple making kissy faces at one another. Despite appearances to the contrary, Snookums and Hunny-Bunny are racked with existential doubt.

If we really are all alone, then it follows that we must take responsibility for our actions. Battling sexual oppression through Gandhi's technique of passive resistance isn't work-ing. We require persistence *and* patience. We need to over-come the anxieties that prevent us from acting on our (hope-fully noble) urges.

> *Reasons not to ask her out: 1,574,894*
>
> *Reasons to ask her out: one. She might say yes.*

Fear is a dark room where negatives get developed. We *must* take risks. Ironic detachment is no longer "cool." Being earnest isn't a bad thing and sarcastically saying "I love you' is now a venal sin. Excessive vulnerability isn't attractive though. We must imitate the action of the tiger; stiffen the sinews, summon up the blood, disguise fair nature with hard-favored rage. Or at least hard-favored courage. Be reasonably confident without succumbing to Ego Inflammation. Remember what Cusack taught us: *I'm Lloyd Dobler.*

A journey of a thousand miles begins with a single step. A date with Ione Skye begins with a single phone call.

Speaking of Ms. Skye, we might want to reassess our stan-dards. A better-than-nothing-relationship is neither, but hid-ing behind a ridiculous must-have list is silly. There are big differences between essential and desirable traits. If a woman you (nearly) fancy prefers Lemon Jif to regular, consider let-ting the matter slide.

We might be as rational as Spock, but we're also as spon-taneous. Flying to New York was, to put it mildly, dumb, but to reiterate an earlier theorem, *I don't regret having done it.* Leanne, the train-tracks woman I had a crush on in high school – well, let's just say I've spent more time than the Warren Commission trying to figure out what went wrong.

There is no magic bullet that will solve our woes. Some guys need only to make minor recalibrations to their dating techniques, others require a complete overhaul. The important thing is to try something different, and try it soon.

Now is the time to ask that woman who works at the library to go for a coffee.

Now is the time to ask the new secretary in Accounting if she'd like to see a movie this Saturday.

Now is the time on Sprockets when we dance.

I say to you today, my friends, that in spite of all our difficulties and frustrations, I still have a dream. It involves the Women's Basketball Association and a Mr. Turtle pool filled with lime Jell-O.

I also have another, more attainable dream: that one day soon, we will find the perfect blend of Astute and Brute. We don't have to sacrifice the things that make us good guys, but a spritz or two of Eau de Brute is acceptable. We shall conquer our quirks and sweep them aside – and a relationship will be ours! *A relationship will be ours!* A RELATIONSHIP WILL BE OURS!

It's a jungle out there. Believe me, I know. I still haven't found a Very Lonely Planet escape hatch, but I have maximized my productivity during the last few years. Some might find this book noble and inspiring; others might view it as a bizarre make-work project. But lest you dare suggest I'm a loser, please remember you paid twenty bucks for the privilege of reading about *my* life. Clearly, I'm doing something right.

Ryan poses for *Teen Beet*
(the magazine for rural adolescents)

About the author:

Ryan Bigge is one of the tallest
freelance writers in Toronto *and* a
former Managing Editor of *Adbusters*.

His writing has appeared in
the *National Post, Toronto Life,
Marketing, This, Broken Pencil,
Ben is Dead,* and *Chunklet.*

For further information about
A Very Lonely Planet,
please visit biggeworld.com